Simple, Heartfelt Words

Preaching in the Alphonsian Tradition

Dennis J. Billy, C.Ss.R.

Liguori, Missouri

Imprimi Potest:
Thomas D. Picton, C.Ss.R.
Provincial, Denver Province
The Redemptorists

Published by Liguori Publications
Liguori, Missouri
www.liguori.org

Parts of this book were previously published as: "Simple, Heartfelt Words: Alphonsus on Preaching," *Spiritus Patris* 30 (no. 1, 2004): 11–15.

Library of Congress Cataloging-in-Publication Data

Billy, Dennis Joseph.
Simple, heartfelt words : preaching in the Alphonsian tradition / Dennis J. Billy.—1st ed.
p. cm.
Includes bibliographical references.
ISBN 0-7648-1376-5 (pbk.)
1. Catholic preaching. 2. Liguori, Alfonso Maria de, Saint, 1696–1787. I. Title.

BX1795.P72B55 2006
251—dc22 2005044990

Liguori Publications, a nonprofit corporation, is an apostolate of the Redemptorists. To learn more about the Redemptorists, visit *Redemptorists.com.*

Printed in the United States of America
10 09 08 07 06 5 4 3 2 1
First edition

For Joseph W. Oppitz, C.Ss.R.
In appreciation

…words alone speak to the ears, but do not enter the soul. He only who speaks from the heart, that is, he who feels and practices what he preaches, shall speak to the heart of others, and shall move them to the love of God.

ALPHONSUS DE LIGUORI

Contents

INTRODUCTION

In his lifetime, Alphonsus de Liguori (1696–1787) was known for many things: bishop, founder of a missionary institute, distinguished moral theologian, renowned confessor, popular spiritual and devotional writer, and teacher of prayer. Early on in his priestly ministry, he also gained a reputation as an accomplished preacher. In many ways, preaching was his lifeblood, the activity to which he dedicated his life and focused most of his apostolic energies. Preaching, for Alphonsus, was a primary means through which people could be encouraged to undergo *metanoia,* or fundamental conversion. Through preaching, he sought to help people turn their lives over to God by calling them to a radical change of heart. To this end, he dedicated the efforts of his missionary congregation, the Redemptorists, the specific purpose of which was to preach the Gospel to the poor and most abandoned.

This book will examine Alphonsus's teaching on preaching. It will do so by looking briefly at the historical context in which he developed it (chapter 1), examining in chronological order a number of key Alphonsian texts (chapters 2—6), and making appropriate adaptations to the situation today (chapter 7). Each chapter opens with a relevant quotation and closes with a series of reflection questions designed to help readers probe Alphonsus's teaching and discover its significance for their own ministry. The aim is to immerse readers in Alphonsus's teaching and help them to translate it in suitable ways for their own circumstances.

A teaching's greatest strength often lies in its ability to adapt to change. To reach this stage of resiliency, however, the foundational texts of that teaching need critical examination, especially with regard to the specific issues being responded to and reacted against. Alphonsus's teaching on preaching is no exception. Only when it is understood in its original historical context can pertinent questions even begin to be asked about its relevance for today. This book seeks to take a small first step in that direction. Although it makes no claim to being a comprehensive treatment of Alphonsus's teaching (either in its historical foundation or application), it offers key elements for consideration to those who carry out their preaching ministry in his spirit and who wish to make it more accessible for preachers of God's Word today.

Chapter One

SOME HISTORICAL BACKGROUND

Oh, why have we so many panegyrics, which invariably terminate in a vain display of talent and ingenious subtleties, devised by volatile imaginations, unintelligible to the people? Let a panegyric, if intended to be useful, be composed in that popular and intelligible style of eloquence which instructs and moves the ignorant no less than the learned; but this is oftentimes not understood by him who fancies himself more learned than others.

LOUIS MURATORI, *CHRISTIAN CHARITY*

Saint Alphonsus de Liguori (1696–1787), founder of the Redemptorist Congregation, doctor of prayer, and patron saint of confessors and moral theologians, was also considered one the preeminent preachers of his day. His approach to preaching was intimately bound to his deep sense of mission to the poor and most abandoned. In his day, he wanted to bring the Gospel message of plentiful redemption to those who lived in the remote hill country of southern Italy in the kingdom of Naples and who, because of their poverty and distance from population centers, had scant access to the Church's rich sacramental life.

ALPHONSUS AND EXTRAORDINARY PREACHING

For Alphonsus, the lack of availability of the simplest and most ordinary means of salvation called for extraordinary measures. His response to the situation he encountered was to gather a band of followers who would conduct missions in the backward, isolated areas of the kingdom. He and his small but fervent group would go where no one else wanted to go. They would preach fundamental conversion to those who had lost touch with the faith or never been properly introduced to it. Through their preaching, they would encourage their hearers to nurture their relationship with God through prayer, the sacraments (especially confession and Eucharist), and devotional practices designed to keep their faith burning long after the conclusion of the mission. They would also return to these small mountain villages from time to time to encourage the people in their faith and to forestall any tendencies toward backsliding.

"Faith comes from what is heard, and what is heard comes through the word of Christ" (Romans 10:17). If Christ and his Word were the lifeblood of Alphonsus and his small band of missionaries, then preaching was the primary means by which they shared that lifeblood with others. For this reason, Alphonsus took special care to instruct the members of the Congregation in the intricate details of effective preaching. Central to his teaching was an insistence that Redemptorist missionaries speak simply, clearly, and from the heart. As strange as it might seem today, this approach went against the general practice of the time and met with substantial pockets of resistance.

To appreciate Alphonsus's teaching, it would be helpful to take a brief look at the history of Christian preaching to the eighteenth century and to outline some of the practices in the kingdom of Naples against which he reacted. The purpose in doing so is not to offer an exhaustive historical presentation of the ministry, but to set the stage for a fuller assessment of Alphonsus's approach.

A Brief Overview

Christian preaching has its origins in Jesus' proclamation of the kingdom and had precursors in the ministry of John the Baptist and the Old Testament prophets. Jesus proclaimed his message publicly and to anyone who would listen. He did so in the synagogues of Galilee, in the open air, and even in the temple in Jerusalem. His words and parables were closely linked to his love for the Father and the call he discerned to lay down his life for his people (cf. John 15:13). Jesus' preaching ultimately led to the *via crucis* and the proclamation of his resurrection by his earliest disciples (cf. Luke 24:34).

After the events of Pentecost, his disciples proclaimed the kerygmatic message of his passion, death, and resurrection. They proclaimed it first to their Jewish brethren in the synagogues and open spaces of first-century Palestine and later to the Gentiles in the surrounding areas and beyond. Little survives of this early kerygmatic preaching other than the material that has been reworked and made its way into the New Testament canon. By far, the greatest preacher of the apostolic period was the apostle Paul. His three missionary journeys and his final journey in captivity gave him the opportunity to preach the gospel throughout much of the Hellenic world. Through his preaching, he gained many converts to the faith and established loosely organized church structures that would continue his work after he left. Many others contributed to the early missionary efforts of the fledgling movement. Within a short time, vibrant Christian communities existed at Jerusalem, Syria, Asia Minor, and Greece. The apostle Peter carried the Gospel to Italy and became the head of the church at Rome. Although the original language of the early Christian preaching was Aramaic, it quickly turned to Greek as the religion spread throughout the Hellenic world and the number of Gentile converts outpaced those of Jewish heritage.

At the beginning of the second century, Christianity spread at a rapid pace throughout the Hellenic world and underwent a transformation of its governing structures and liturgical worship. These changes in Church order and worship had consequences for the ministry of Christian preaching. One scholar notes four important changes: "...(a) a transition in the notion of preacher from charismatic prophet to hierarchic priest, (b) an equally significant change in the notion of worship from Jewish *synaxis* to Christian Eucharist, (c) a totally new form of exegesis from Jewish allegory to Christian typology, and (d) a new style of presentation as classical rhetoric replaces biblical diatribe."[1] Although exceptions certainly existed, it is fair to say that, with the spread of Christianity in the Hellenic world, the ministry of preaching became closely associated with the emergence of the hierarchical priesthood and the celebration of the Eucharist. Although thinkers such as Origen (d. 250), Augustine of Hippo (d. 430), and John Cassian (d. 435) maintained and even developed the allegorical method of exegesis, other Christian preachers such as Diodorus of Tarsus (d. c. 390) and Theodore of Mopsuestia (d. 428) searched the Jewish Scriptures for Christian typology rooted in the literal meaning of the text. While the allegorical method of biblical interpretation flourished in Alexandria, this typological approach became firmly rooted in Antioch.

Yet another important influence on Christian preaching during this period was its adaptation to classical Greco-Roman rhetoric. As the Church adapted itself to Hellenic culture and entered into the higher, more educated social strata, its preachers employed the art of persuasion to deepen the faith of their hearers. In the Greek East, the Cappadocian fathers, Basil the Great (d. 379), Gregory Nazianzus (d. c. 390), Gregory of Nyssa (d. c. 395), and John Chrysostom (d. 407), inspired their audiences with homilies, panegyrics, sermons, catecheses, and funeral orations. In the Latin West, Ambrose of Milan (d. 397) and Augustine of Hippo did much the same with their exegetical homilies, and topical sermons. Augustine's influence on

Christian preaching is especially noteworthy for the history of preaching. Book four of his *De doctrina Christiana* represents the first Latin treatise on the subject, providing guidelines that would influence the ministry in western Christianity for the rest of late antiquity. In his *Moralia*, Gregory the Great (d. 604) emphasized the moral and pastoral dimensions of these teachings and was important for spreading their influence throughout the Latin West.

During the early Middle Ages of western Europe, preaching was primarily in Latin, a phenomenon due in part because the vernacular languages were still emerging and had not yet found their way into a written format. The influence of Augustine dominates this period. Many of the more noted preachers of this time made collections of homilies and sermons to help the clergy in the exercise of their ministry. One of the most important changes in this period of Church history is the decree by the Council of Tours in 817, which instructed bishops to give homilies for the instruction of the faithful. This decree necessitated the translation of homilies in the vernacular. The use of the vernacular became increasingly important in the medieval period, especially for the preaching of the Crusades in the twelfth and thirteenth centuries.

With the rise and rapid growth of scholasticism and the appearance of the mendicant orders, especially the Franciscans and Dominicans, Christian preaching developed in two ways. At the university level, the scholastic sermon was typically written in Latin and used syllogistic logic to prove a point of Christian teaching. On the popular level, however, preachers used the vernacular to touch the hearts of the people in practical ways that affected their daily lives. The Franciscan and Dominican Orders had experts in both kinds of preaching. They excelled at the university, but also proved an effective counterbalance to the popular preaching of heretical sects such as the Humiliati and Waldensians. The popular mendicant preachers emulated these groups by preaching in the open air.

During the Renaissance, preaching continued to be a major

source of church activity. With the invention of the printing press, sermons were more widely available and given greater diffusion than their manuscript or oral presentation. Mission preaching became extremely popular as a way of renewing the faith of the faithful. In emphasizing the power of God's Word over the sacraments, the Protestant Reformation gave priority of place to the ministry of preaching in the worship of the Christian faithful. The Council of Trent closely aligned preaching with the office of bishop and insisted on its frequent exercise and the teaching of the rudiments of the faith. After Trent, the Church established a seminary system that gave priority to sound priestly training in the theological disciplines, in the celebration of the sacraments, and in the ministry of preaching. It also commissioned orders such as the Franciscans, Dominicans, and Jesuits to bring the Gospel to foreign lands and to strengthen the faithful at home through Lenten preaching and popular missions. In the seventeenth and eighteenth centuries, the Church continued to promote the aims of the Counter Reformation, and the preacher became an important vehicle of its program of reform. It now sought to frustrate not only the efforts of the Protestant churches but also the rising tide of the Enlightenment. In Italy, missionary societies, such as the Pious Workers and the Apostolic Missions, and missionary congregations, such as the Vincentians, Passionists, and Redemptorists, played an important role in the ongoing popular renewal of the faith.[2]

ALPHONSUS'S APPROACH

The kingdom of Naples during the eighteenth century was affected by a complex mixture of Enlightened reform that was compounded by the anti-Roman attitudes of the ruling Bourbon nobility and a highly stratified class consciousness rooted in the feudal culture that had influenced the southern Italian peninsula for centuries. Into this highly volatile sense of class-consciousness, the ministry of preaching took on different shapes to address the sensibilities of the various classes. For Alphonsus, many of the preachers of his day placed a disproportionate amount of effort into speaking to the higher, more educated elements of society. Preachers had adopted chantlike tones and elaborate periodic constructions to please the aesthetic sensibilities of their listeners. They invoked imagery and symbolism from Greek and Roman mythology that would be recognized only by a highly refined literary mind. These practices were most often found in panegyrics and funeral orations, but eventually found their way into regular, nonoccasional preaching.

Alphonsus reacted strongly against such practices. Although he refused to judge the motivations of these preachers, he insisted that their words went over the heads of most hearers and tended to draw attention not to God, but to themselves. What is more, by focusing on the educated classes, these preachers were ignoring the impoverished classes, those for whom Jesus had a special love and tenderness. Strongly influenced by the study of popular eloquence by Louis Muratori (d. 1750), Alphonsus insisted on expounding the Scriptures in simple, heartfelt words that even the most uneducated person in the audience could understand. The challenge of preaching, for Alphonsus, was not to draw attention to oneself by impressing one's hearers with one's gift of eloquence, but to break open the bread of God's Word so that it could give nourishment to as many people as possible, especially the poor and most abandoned.

Alphonsus both democratizes and personalizes the preaching ministry for the people of his day. He seeks to return to the apostolic witness of Jesus' earliest followers who spoke simply, but powerfully in a way that moved the hearts of their hearers to give their lives to Jesus Christ. Preaching, for him, must never exclude a particular class or social element. Although he recognizes the importance of rhetoric, he wants it to be a type that invites all of those listening to open their hearts to the Word. He stands in the long tradition of popular preaching that has its roots in the apostolic era and that threaded its way through the Church's history in itinerant vernacular movements that moved people to strengthen their personal commitment to Christ. In every aspect of his ministry—his spiritual and moral writings, his confessional practice, the founding of the Congregation—Alphonsus used his education to serve his people, not to impress them. This statement is especially true for the way he conducted his ministry of preaching.[3]

OBSERVATIONS

Alphonsus's approach to preaching invites careful examination so that his followers today might adapt it appropriately to their own situations. The following areas of concern deserve special attention.

1. Alphonsus's approach to preaching was thoroughly *apostolic*. From the earliest day of Christianity, preaching involved a twofold function: the following of Christ and going forth to preach the Good News. Alphonsus considered these two facets of the apostolic life intimately related. Preachers' lives and the message they bear must be firmly rooted in Christ. To drive a wedge between the two, to separate or divorce them in any way, is harmful to the preachers themselves, their message, and their listeners. In order to preach Christ, today's apostolic preachers must dedicate themselves entirely to the following of Christ. If they do not, their words will have little force and even less effect. No one will listen to them, because they themselves do not put into practice the very message they preach.

2. Alphonsus saw the *need for rhetoric* in the ministry of preaching and wanted his followers to be thoroughly skilled in the art of persuasion. He was also keenly aware of the danger it represented, and he exhorted preachers to use the skill as a means of drawing attention to God, not themselves. For this reason, he instructed preachers to speak simply, honestly, and from the heart. To do so required a great deal of preparation and practice. Alphonsus would have had little time for those who would give these up in the name of spontaneous emotional outpourings. True spontaneity requires intense study and prayerful reflection.

Those who neglect their responsibilities in this regard can easily confuse the inspirations of the Spirit with their own feelings and, worse yet, their own latent laziness. For the Spirit to speak through preachers, it was necessary for them to break open God's Word and ruminate upon its hidden mysteries.

3. Alphonsus's approach to preaching was also thoroughly *popular*. Preaching, for him, was a primary way of reaching out to the poor and most abandoned. He was especially conscious of the audience he was addressing and wanted to make sure that even the simple and uneducated could understand him. When written and delivered well, a homily or sermon should be beneficial to all classes of people, regardless of their education or social status. Alphonsus sought to display the naked truth of the Gospel. That truth does not distinguish between rich and poor, noble and peasant, educated and uneducated. It penetrates the heart and puts a person in touch with his or her innermost poverty before God. Popular preaching, for Alphonsus, brings a person face to face with the call to fundamental conversion. It seeks to put the audience in touch with their common humanity and radical need for God.

4. Alphonsus's preaching, moreover, was *enculturated*. He sought a basic knowledge of the attitudes and customs of his listeners and then presented his message in a way that would connect with them and win over their hearts. Doing so did not mean a watering down of the Gospel message, but a prudent application of its essential values to the situation of the faithful. It required on Alphonsus's part a capacity to distinguish the essential from the nonessential in the Gospel proclamation and to distill those positive values and practices in a particular locality that he could emphasize in a homily or sermon as a way of reaching out and showing that Christ was Emmanuel, "God with us." From there, he sought to celebrate Christ's presence in the midst of the community and then emphasize what more they needed to do to turn their lives over totally to God.

5. Finally, Alphonsus sees an intimate connection between preaching and *prayer*. Preachers' words should arise not only

from study but also from prayerful reflection on the words of Scripture. Preachers, moreover, should ask God for guidance throughout the entire process of preparation, practice, and delivery of a sermon. They should view the ministry of preaching as a vibrant extension of their lives of prayer. As the "doctor of prayer," Alphonsus emphasized the importance preachers should give to helping people deepen their relationship with God through prayer. "He who prays is certainly saved," he liked to say.[4] He believed that helping people to pray was one of the primary goals of preaching. Only by arousing in people a desire for God and providing them with concrete ways of opening their hearts to him will they make any progress in the spiritual life.

These observations point out the relevance of Alphonsus's approach for today. While not exhaustive, they highlight some very basic areas where preachers can benefit from his understanding of what it means to proclaim Christ's message of love and forgiveness. If nothing else, they remind us that the Gospel message is a two-edged sword, one that challenges both preacher and hearer alike to open their hearts and dedicate themselves to a life of fundamental conversion.

CONCLUSION

In his day, Alphonsus had a great reputation for sanctity and for the power of his preaching. For him, the two were closely related; standing before a public audience to proclaim the Good News of Jesus' death and resurrection required humility, honesty, courage, and prayer. It also demanded a sense of proportion and evenhandedness so one part of the congregation is not unduly favored over another. Alphonsus leveled the playing field of the preaching ministry by seeking to make sure that everyone had access to good, solid preaching, regardless of their background, social status, or geographical location. He democratized the ministry by simplifying the content and shape of his preaching so that the naked truth of the Gospel would break through his words and touch the hearts of rich and poor alike.

Even when being focused on everyone present, however, Alphonsus knew that effective preaching meant turning to God for help at every moment of the process (preparation, practice, delivery, and so on). He knew that preachers must humbly ask the Lord to speak through them if their listeners were to open their hearts and be moved to change. He knew that if preachers did not take the time to nourish an intimate relationship with the Lord, their listeners would see through them and fail to respond. He also knew that preachers speak first with the actions of their lives and only secondarily with their words.

What Alphonsus knew, he also put into action. His approach to preaching was intimately tied to his sense of mission. He believed that no one ever stood still in his or her relationship with God. He used simple, heartfelt words with a sense of urgency that confronted his hearers with a fundamental choice: to draw closer to God or to turn away from God. For him, the whole purpose of preaching was to do whatever was necessary to help a person foster an intimate relationship with Christ. Aware of his inability to bring about such a change in the lives of his hearers, he relied heavily on the power of God's grace to open the hearts and transform the lives of his listeners. Alphonsus saw himself in the people he served. Without Christ, he knew that everyone was poor and abandoned. With Christ, all were assured of plentiful redemption and the fullness of life. To this end, he directed his preaching and dedicated his entire life.

Reflection Questions

1. Have you learned anything about the ministry of preaching from the brief overview of its history presented in this chapter? Which period in the history of preaching inspires you the most? Does any period of this history trouble or disturb you? What lessons should preachers take from the history of their ministry? How would you describe the present historical status of the ministry? Where is the ministry going? How is it developing?

2. What is your understanding of Alphonsus's mission of extraordinary preaching to the poor and most abandoned? Do you understand it? Do you agree with it? What does it mean today? Does it need to be adapted? How would you apply it? How would you implement it? Who are the poor and most abandoned in your local area? How is the Gospel being shared with them? How would Alphonsus approach them?
3. When you think of the phrase "apostolic preaching," what models or images come to mind? The apostles? The fathers of the Church? Some of the great saints who were known for their preaching apostolate? In what sense did Alphonsus consider his preaching to be "apostolic"? Upon whom did he model his preaching? Whom did he try to emulate? Do you find his approach to preaching inspiring? If so, why?
4. In what sense did Alphonsus "democratize" the ministry of preaching in the eighteenth-century kingdom of Naples? Do you think what he did was right? Do you think it was successful? What is the ministry of preaching most in need of today? Does it need to be "democratized"? If so, in what sense? Who are the ones being excluded from hearing the Word of God today? What can be done to turn things around?
5. What does it mean to enculturate the preaching of the Gospel in a given situation? How did Alphonsus do it? What concrete methods did he use? Would those methods still work today? Do they need to be adapted? Does preaching mean the same as it did in the time of Alphonsus? Does it have the same effect? What kind of preaching is most effective in a culture flooded with images and sound bites?

Chapter Two

SOME GENERAL CHARACTERISTICS

Greater attention is to be given to speak with fervor, and with a hunger for souls, and with a desire in every sermon to sanctify the entire audience, and the entire world, if this were possible.

"CONSTITUTION ON SIMPLICITY AND MANNER OF PREACHING"

One of the first places where we can find a clearly thought-out presentation of the characteristics of Redemptorist preaching is in a brief document of the General Chapter of October 1747 entitled, "Constitution on Simplicity and Manner of Preaching."[1] Although the Congregation's secretary attached his name to the document, it is not clear who exactly penned it or to what extent the chapter delegates actually treated it. Since its central theme is one that appears many times in Alphonsus's published writings and literary correspondence, it would be fair to assume that he influenced its composition to some extent and may even have written it himself.[2] A look at its contents will give us a good idea of how, from very early on, the early Redemptorist missionaries understood their preaching ministry within the Church.

THE PURPOSE AND MANNER OF PREACHING

The Constitution's opening paragraph focuses on the purpose and manner of preaching. The purpose of preaching is twofold: to propagate and preserve the faith of Christ. To do so effectively, one must preach in the manner of Jesus Christ and his apostles. Only in this way will people be converted and find their way to God. To back up its claim, the Constitution refers to a number of passages from Saint Paul, the preacher par excellence of the early Church (cf. Romans 10:14, 17; 1 Corinthians 2:4). Paul is the apostle who spread the faith and conserved it in the early Church by relying not on the persuasive force of "wise" argumentation, but on the power of the Spirit. In like manner, Redemptorists are encouraged to preach the Gospel by following the example of Christ and his apostles. Like them, they must preach humbly, simply, and from the heart.[3]

Following these opening remarks come a number of references from Catholic authors who have written on the manner of preaching and its effectiveness. The venerable Father Master Avila accuses those who preach with vanity of being "traitors of Jesus Christ." Father Caspar Sanzio, in turn, calls them "persecutors of the Church," for they cause many souls to be lost. Saint Francis of Sales calls them "pests," because they preach not to move the wills of their hearers, but merely to show off their intellects. "Experience," the Constitution asserts, "shows that souls do not change their lives with such preaching, because God does not cooperate with vanity."[4]

The Constitution then tells the members of the Congregation that they must be especially dedicated to the imitation of Christ and his apostles. When they care for the people in the country, they must break the bread of the word not with chant-like tones or with vanity of words or ideas, but in an apostolic manner that is clear, simple, familiar, and popular. They are to preach Christ Crucified with fervor, with a hunger for souls, and with a desire in every sermon to sanctify the whole congregation and even the entire world. Preaching in this way, the

Constitution goes on, is not a matter of choice, but of conscience. They are warned not to corrupt the simplicity of the preaching that has its roots in apostolic practice and which the Congregation has used to help so many people draw closer to God.[5]

The superiors of the Congregation are then charged, as a matter of conscience, to regulate the preaching of the members of their communities: "They are never to allow, at any time or in any place, a subject of the Congregation to preach in any other way."[6] They are told that they themselves are responsible for ensuring that both the content and style of the preaching within the Congregation are sound and beyond reproach. If they are negligent in this task, they will have to render an account to Jesus himself. The Constitution wishes to avoid infecting the way Redemptorist missionaries preach: "Once profane preaching has been introduced and permitted..., it can be eradicated later only with great difficulty."[7] It concludes by obligating superiors to take strong exemplary measures against those who because of stubbornness go against this rule. If there is no hope of change, they are to forbid such transgressors ever to preach again.[8]

The Characteristics of Redemptorist Preaching

Short as it is, this Constitution contains the main elements of the Redemptorist approach to the preaching ministry. The following list of characteristics is arranged in their order of appearance in the document.

1. *Conversion of Souls.* The goal of preaching is to spread the faith and preserve it by seeking the conversion of their listeners. Wherever they go, Redemptorists are called to invite their hearers to believe in the Good News of Jesus Christ. They must also sustain the faith of those who already do believe and strive to deepen it. They must never lose sight of this purpose. Otherwise, they will use their preaching not to lead others to Christ, but to build up themselves and their own reputations.

2. *Rooted in Word and Spirit.* Redemptorist preaching must

be rooted in both Scripture and the power of the Spirit. The Constitution uses quotations from Paul's Letter to the Romans and First Letter to the Corinthians to emphasize both the importance of preaching for the spread of the Gospel and the need to rely on the power of the Spirit rather than the powers of persuasion and worldly argumentation. In like manner, Redemptorists must base their preaching on the revealed Word of God and trust in the Spirit to lead others to experience a fundamental change of heart.

3. *Imitating Christ.* In their preaching, Redemptorists seek to follow the example of Christ. They want to preach the way Jesus and his disciples did. They follow in the footsteps of Christ by embracing a missionary lifestyle that highlights the ministry of preaching to the poor and abandoned. Their distinctive vocation in the Church hinges on imitating Christ in this way. Doing so is not a question of style or personal choice, but a vital necessity to the people they serve and their own personal and communal sanctification.

4. *Rooted in Tradition.* Redemptorists also seek to root their preaching in the living tradition of the Church. The Constitution makes a number of references to revered saints and spiritual authors, who point out the dangers of vanity for preachers of God's Word. In like manner, Redemptorists must be well versed in the Church's teachings and spiritual writings so that they will be ready and able to cite in their sermons appropriate examples with which they can inspire their listeners.

5. *Breaking Open the Bread of the Word.* In their preaching, Redemptorists seek to open up the meaning of the Scriptures so that the Gospel message can be applied to the lives of their listeners in meaningful and relevant ways. The Word of God is meant to bring spiritual nourishment to those who hear it. Redemptorist preachers must ponder the Scriptures so that they can make that nourishment readily available to God's people. For this to happen, they must spend time with the Word of God in prayer so that they might receive nourishment from it for their own personal lives.

6. *Preaching Christ Crucified.* Redemptorists preach Christ crucified, "a stumbling block to Jews and foolishness to Gentiles" (1 Corinthians 1:23). The Gospel message has its roots in Jesus laying down his life for the salvation of the world. The power of this message, however, does not end with Jesus' death on the cross, but points beyond it to the empty tomb. Redemptorists preach the whole Gospel, not just a part of it. They preach a message of plentiful redemption rooted in the Christ event and oriented toward the fullness of life that Christ's death and resurrection from the dead has made possible for all.

7. *An Apostolic Manner.* The Constitution insists that Redemptorists preach in an apostolic manner. Positively speaking, this means preaching the way Christ and his apostles did. Negatively speaking, it means avoiding any use of the pulpit for one's own self-aggrandizement. For this reason, Redemptorist preachers must avoid the use of eloquent tones and sophisticated arguments that turn their hearers' attention to them rather than to Christ. Rhetorical vanity, of whatever kind, is directly opposed to the manner of apostolic preaching. Redemptorists must do all in their power to avoid such pitfalls.

8. *A Simple Style.* To be even more specific, the Constitution lists four particular characteristics of the Redemptorist preaching style. It must be clear, simple, familiar, and popular. Their message must be unambiguous, easy for everyone to understand, easily digestible, and capable of a wide diffusion. Redemptorists aim their message toward the masses, not the select few. They use simple, unsophisticated language to reach as many people as possible. These characteristics form the trademark of the Redemptorist style. They are not to be tampered or played with for the sake of drawing attention to oneself or making a good impression.

9. *With Heartfelt Fervor.* In their preaching, Redemptorists are also called to speak from the heart. Before preaching, they must carefully reflect upon God's Word and ponder it in their hearts. Only by doing so will they themselves be convinced that their message has value for their hearers and needs to be heard.

Preaching, for them, is something that they must feel compelled to do. If God's Word has not taken root in their own hearts, they will be unable to speak with fervor and convince their hearers that their words have any direct relevance for their lives. Lukewarm preachers preach lukewarm sermons and achieve lukewarm results. They fail to draw others closer to Christ, because they themselves are not convinced that their words really can make a difference in their listeners' lives.

10. *A Desire to Sanctify.* Redemptorists preach in order to draw others closer to God. They prepare and deliver their sermons with that end in mind. They desire holiness for their listeners and firmly believe that God has brought them together at this particular place and time to achieve that end. Redemptorists believe in the universal call to holiness. They extend this invitation to holiness so that all might become members of the communion of saints. They desire their own sanctity and the sanctity of their listeners. Despite their awareness of their own sinfulness and that of their listeners, they firmly believe in the power of God's transforming love. With God, they believe, all things are possible (cf. Mark 10:27).

11. *A Matter of Conscience.* The Constitution presents its teaching on the simplicity and manner of preaching as a matter of conscience. Redemptorists are strongly exhorted not to change a style of preaching that goes back to the very beginning and that, as practiced in the Congregation, has done much good for so very many people. To avoid doing unnecessary harm to the Church's missionary efforts, this simple apostolic style should not be tampered with. By making the Redemptorist style of preaching a matter of conscience, the Constitution places the ministry of preaching soundly in the area of moral responsibility. Every Redemptorist preacher has the responsibility to communicate God's Word to his people in as simple, clear, and heartfelt manner as possible.

12. *A Communal Responsibility.* The Constitution also presents the preservation of this particular style of preaching as the responsibility of the community. It does so by reminding

Redemptorist superiors of their responsibility to ensure that the confreres follow the norms for preaching adopted by the Congregation. Superiors are to put in place special safeguards that will prevent the community from deviating from these simple guidelines. Failure to do so could have a disastrous effect on the community's life and apostolic mission.

Observations

When taken together, the above characteristics offer a general description of the traditional Redemptorist approach to the ministry of preaching. The following five observations seek to expand upon this description by making relevant adaptations to the situation of Redemptorist preachers in the world today.

1. To begin with, the Redemptorist emphasis on conversion needs to take into account the various levels of human existence: the physical, the emotion, the intellectual, the social, and the spiritual—to name just a few. If in the past they focused primarily on the *metanoia,* or change, in the individual, their preaching today should strive to strike a balance between personal conversion and the need for social justice. The close, intimate relationship between the individual and his or her social environment requires preachers to be sensitive to the way these dimensions interact and affect each other. Sometimes, the best way one can uphold the dignity of the human person is to strive to create social conditions that would be conducive to the authentic human and spiritual growth of the individual.

2. The strong emphasis on inculturation in the Church today should lead Redemptorist preachers to examine the underlying cultural prejudices that inform their own preaching and to do what they can to adapt their manner and style to the cultural mores of their listeners. The meaning of such basic values as "clarity," "simplicity," and "familiarity" can vary from one culture to the next. Redemptorists should take care that the underlying values that guide the style and manner of their preaching are adapted to the culture in which they minister. Alphonsus

himself was keenly aware of the need for Redemptorists to adapt the manner and style of their preaching from one situation to the next. Today's Redemptorist preachers should take into account the cultural mind-set of their listeners and do all they can to present the Gospel message in a way that they can easily hear, understand, and take to heart.

3. Because of the strong authoritarian structure of Redemptorist community life in the time of Saint Alphonsus, the Constitution places much of the burden on safeguarding the standards of Redemptorist preaching on the shoulders of superiors. Since the structures of Redemptorist community life have become much more democratic since the close of Vatican Council II and the final revision of the Redemptorist *Constitutions and Statutes* in 1983, it would seem that the responsibility must now be much more a shared one. Giving *everyone* this important responsibility, however, can also be a subtle way of giving it to *no one*. To avoid this danger, the community should develop structures of coresponsibility that enable the community to take a careful look at both the content and style of its preaching. Periodic workshops, weekly reflection groups, and other such structures can help the members of the community to take ownership of their responsibility to preach God's Word to the people they serve boldly, clearly, and without restraint.

4. Today, Redemptorist preachers also need to be sensitive to the historical dimensions of the Gospel they preach. In their desire to draw others toward God, they need to be aware that the Church's understanding of what it means to lead a holy, sanctified life has been conditioned by a variety of factors in its earthly sojourn. "Holiness" is not a monolithic concept that has remained unchanged from one historical epoch to the next. To verify this claim, one need only examine the different models of discipleship that have captured the Christian imagination from one historical period to another. Redemptorist preachers need to be keenly aware of what it means to be holy at the dawn of the third millennium. The current emphasis in the Church on the universal call to holiness should encourage them

to be sensitive to the variety of paths to sanctity in the Church today. It should also help them to avoid those elitist, hierarchical concepts encouraged in the past that singled out a particular vocation as a holier way of life than others (for example, priestly and religious life over the laity).

5. Finally, regardless of their historical situation, Redemptorist preachers must be men of deep prayer. The words they preach to others must come from their own personal relationship to the Word of God. If they are not, they will not be sincere in what they say and their hearers will be able to sense it. Prayer is not an accessory to successful preaching, but a fundamental prerequisite for it. If Redemptorist preachers do not pray, they will never be able to follow in the footsteps of the Lord along the way of holiness. If they are not walking along this path, they will never be able to convince others to do so. Alphonsus exhorted his confreres many times about the importance of preaching on prayer as "the great means of salvation." It is impossible to preach effectively on such a topic, if the preacher has not himself benefited from the fruits of a rich prayer life.

These remarks point to the need for adapting the Redemptorist charism of preaching to changing cultures and historical circumstances. At the same time, they also encourage members of the Congregation to be rooted in the tradition of Alphonsus so that the good news of plentiful redemption in Christ will continue to reach the poor and abandoned of this world. While these observations do not exhaust the ways in which the characteristics of Redemptorist preaching found in the Constitution of 1747 must be adapted to the present moment, they offer a general framework of thought to reinterpret and apply the tradition presented in the document to very different circumstances.

Conclusion

The "Constitution on Simplicity and Manner of Preaching" of 1747 outlines the main characteristics of the Redemptorist preaching ministry. It does so by presenting this ministry as a key way in which the members of the Congregation follow in the footsteps of Christ. Redemptorists are called to preach as Christ and his disciples did. *Imitatio Christi*, for them, means preaching the Word of God to others in a manner that is clear, simple, familiar, popular, and heartfelt.

In their preaching, Redemptorists must seek to draw attention to Christ and not themselves. To do so, they must avoid needless linguistic displays and complicated lines of argumentation that draw attention more to their own talents than to the gift of salvation being offered their hearers. They must prepare their sermons well, but rely principally on the power of the Spirit to bring about a fundamental conversion in the lives of their listeners.

Above all, Redemptorist preachers must be dedicated men of prayer. If they do not converse with God familiarly in their own hearts, they will be unable to break open God's Word and share it with others. If they cannot break open God's Word and pass on its nourishing truths to their hearers, their preaching will be shallow and ultimately ineffectual. No matter how clear and simple their language may be and no matter how well they may adapt their style of communicating to the cultural milieu in which they are ministering, their preaching will be unconvincing if they themselves do not speak from their own personal experience of God Word resounding in their hearts.

REFLECTION QUESTIONS

1. What, in your opinion, are the primary characteristics of Redemptorist preaching? Do you agree with those listed above? Is there anything you would like to add? Is there anything you would scratch? Are some characteristics more important than others? If so, which ones are they and why? Is there anything particularly distinctive about Redemptorist preaching? If so, what is it and how would you describe it?
2. What does the preaching of fundamental conversion mean today? What should its purpose and function be? How

should the preacher determine which levels of human existence to emphasize? What personal, communal, and societal factors should the preacher take into account? Should the link between fundamental conversion and the struggle for social justice be further developed? If so, how?

3. What does it mean to preach plentiful redemption today? Are there any constants in this concept? If so, what are they and how would you describe them? To what extent does the concept of redemption affect the societal and cultural milieu where the preaching takes place? As the preacher moves about from place to place and even from culture to culture, what factors would merit an adaptation of the content or shape of the message to fit the circumstances? What criteria should the preacher use to distinguish what is essential to the message from what is subject to change?
4. Does the Redemptorist community take responsibility for its preaching? On the worldwide level? On the regional level? On the provincial or vice provincial level? On the local level? What structures have been tried and proven to be successful? What can be done to further this communal responsibility? How should this communal responsibility relate to the individual preacher? What role does fraternal correction play in this call to responsible preaching?
5. How does prayer relate to preaching? Is it central, ancillary, or merely peripheral to the ministry? As it relates to preaching, is it primarily personal or communal? Have you found a particular prayer form to be more helpful than others? If so, do you think this prayer form could be of help to other preachers? If so, how could you share it with them? What role does silence play in your preparation and delivery of a homily or a sermon? What role does *lectio divina* or prayerful reflection? Do you ask God about what you should say and how you should say it?

Chapter Three

A Practical Guide to Preaching

But, to save souls, it is not enough to preach: it is, as I have already said, necessary to preach in a proper manner. In the first place, in order to preach well learning and study are necessary. He who preaches at random will do more injury than service to religion. In the second place, an exemplary life is necessary.

Alphonsus de Liguori, *Selva*

After many years of experience on the missions, Alphonsus collected many of his instructions and sermons in a work called the "Dignity and Duties of the Priest, or Selva" (1760).[1] At one point in this treatise, Alphonsus offers a very clear and practical guide to preaching. These guidelines are brief, easy to remember, and aimed at anyone involved in the Church's ministry of preaching. With appropriate adaptations, they have importance relevance for today and should be reviewed regularly by all actively engaged in the ministry of preaching.

CONTEXT

The *Selva* was directed specifically toward the clergy. It represents the culmination of nearly four decades of work of offering retreats and spiritual exercises to priests throughout the kingdom of Naples. As he states in his opening *Admonitions*, Alphonsus refers to the work as a *selva* (Italian for "forest" or "wood"), because he does not order his material in the form of a regular discourse, nor does he extend his thoughts on any of the subjects.[2] He has merely gathered together the various sermons and instructions he has written for priests over the years and offers them now to a wider reading public. The work can also be used by priests for spiritual reading or for making private retreats.

Alphonsus divides the body of his work into two parts. The first contains sermon material related to the dignity and duty of priests;[3] the second concerns similar material that could be used for conferences.[4] Alphonsus also adds to the work a number of appendices. These deal with such topics as a rule of life for the diocesan priesthood, spiritual rules for priests desiring holiness, a list of spiritual maxims for priests, an exhortation to seminarians, and a discourse on the necessity of making mental prayer.[5]

Alphonsus gives his work this very loose structure for a specific reason. He believes that a preacher will not be able to present material with fervor and zeal if he has not taken the time to make it his own. In the very least, the preacher must select material, arrange it, and extend it through a composition of his own making. Alphonsus offers retreat directors for priests raw material (a veritable forest) from which they can select topics appropriate to the occasion and construct a house that is truly their own. Alphonsus is not interested in providing his readers with a finished set of spiritual exercises that can be consistently applied and repeated, again and again, from one occasion to the next. Instead, he offers them the fruit of his labors and encourages them to go through it and make from it something of their own.

To this end, he adds a series of seven admonitions to his introduction to the work. In the first place, he tells those hoping to give spiritual exercises to priests that they should seek nothing but God's glory and the holiness of their hearers. Second, they should say things that will move the hearts of their hearers and lead them to make some good resolution. Third, they should frequently remind their hearers of the truths of eternity (death, judgment, heaven, hell), because meditating on these truths will most likely lead them to make a change in their lives. Fourth, they should be careful to talk about practical things (for example, the manner of making mental prayer, thanksgiving after Mass, hearing confessions), because, like most people, priests remember only what is practical. Fifth, they should treat the priests listening to them with respect, never putting them on the spot, but always treating them with the kindness and dignity they deserve. Sixth, they must never leave their hearers in despair, but encourage them to hope in the love of Jesus Christ and to recommend to them the exercise of prayer, especially the prayer of petition. Finally, they must expect results not because of their own labors but on account of the mercy of God. To this end, they should pray to God and beg him to give power to their words: "[T]he conversion of priests," he reminds his readers, "must be the fruit of prayer more than study."[6] Although these admonitions are meant specifically for those preaching priest retreats or for spiritual reading for priests, they can be easily adapted to the preaching ministry in general. Later in the *Selva*, Alphonsus actually makes such an adaptation.

ALPHONSUS'S INSTRUCTION ON PREACHING

Alphonsus's general teaching on preaching appears in the fourth instruction of the second part of the treatise.[7] It forms the opening section of a conference devoted to preaching and the administration of the sacrament of penance.[8] For Alphonsus, these two actions number among the priest's most sacred duties: "If all preachers and confessors fulfilled the obligations of their office the whole world would be sanctified. Bad preachers and bad confessors are the ruin of the world. By bad preachers and confessors I mean those that do not fulfill their duty as they ought."[9] Alphonsus treats each of these activities, first preaching and then the administration of the sacrament of penance. We will confine our remarks only to what Alphonsus has to say about the former.

Alphonsus begins his teaching by telling his readers that the faith is both spread and preserved by preaching. It is not enough for Christians merely to know their obligations; they must also hear the Word of God and be reminded of the goal of eternal salvation and of the means of achieving it. He backs this claim up with numerous references from Scripture, most notably the apostle Paul (cf. Romans 10:17; 2 Timothy 4:2) and the prophets Isaiah (cf. 58:1), Jeremiah (cf. 1:9), and Ezechiel (3:18).[10] He also refers to Jesus' injunction to the disciples as recorded in the Gospel of Matthew: "Go therefore and make disciples of all nations...teaching them to obey everything that I have commanded you" (28:19–20). Alphonsus insists, however, that it is not enough merely to preach the Word of God. One must also preach in the proper manner. In the first place, learning and study are necessary, if one is to preach well. Second, it is important that the preacher lead an exemplary life. He backs up these claims with sayings reaped from the Scriptures (cf. Psalm 38:4; Romans 2:1; Matthew 10:27) and reliable teachers of the Christian faith (for example, Gregory the Great, John Chrysostom, Francis de Sales). When these two conditions are combined, "...they form the fiery darts that afterward wound the hearts of their hearers."[11]

Alphonsus also states that it is important to preach with a good intention. One must wish the glory of God and the conversion of one's listeners. The preacher should not hope to receive temporal fruits or to extract empty praises, but only to bring about the salvation of souls. Citing the Council of Trent, he also states that preachers should speak according to the capacity of their hearers. According to Saint Francis de Sales,

"Empty words and sounding periods are the pest of sermons."[12] God does not work through vain preaching. Moreover, the majority of those present are usually simple and illiterate, who do not understand such discourses. He cites Father John d'Avila, who said that those who preach in such a lofty and unintelligible style are traitors to Jesus Christ, since they seek not the glory of God, but their own exaltation. He also cites Father Caspar Sanzio, who identifies these kinds of preachers as the greatest persecutors of the Church. Sermons should be written in a simple, apostolic style. He uses no less of an authority than Saint Paul to back up this claim: "My speech and my proclamation were not with plausible words of wisdom, but with a demonstration of the Spirit and of power" (1 Corinthians 2:4). Many of the saints, Alphonsus says, have been praised for preaching in a simple, popular style. None of them, however, have ever been praised for preaching in an elaborate, eloquent one.[13]

Alphonsus concludes his instruction on preaching with the key points of Louis Muratori's treatise entitled *Popular Eloquence*. Muratori identifies two types of eloquence: sublime and popular. The former, "...directs us in the composition of discourses which treat of lofty subjects, contain ingenious reflections, select language, and turned periods."[14] In the latter, by way of contrast, "...the eternal truths are expounded nakedly, subjects easily understood are explained in a simple and familiar style, so that each person present may understand the entire instruction."[15]

Because both the learned and the simple are often present together at sermons, the preacher should preach in a way that everyone can understand. For this reason, "...it is always expedient to preach in a simple, popular style, not only in the missions and spiritual exercises, but also in all sermons addressed to the people."[16] Everyone will be able to understand such sermons: simple and learned alike. Such sermons, moreover, are more beneficial to the learned than discourses written in an elaborate, flowery style. In such sublime discourses, the mind stops to admire and criticize, but is not left with any food for nourishment. Those who preach in a simple, popular style, by way of contrast, ravish the hearts of all.[17]

According to Muratori, the goal of true rhetoric is "...to persuade and move the audience to practice what is inculcated in the discourse."[18] Even those who preach in a simple, popular style must avail themselves of the art of rhetoric. They must seek to do so simply and without ostentation, so that they draw attention not to themselves, but to God. The goal of the sermon is to reap the fruit of the Spirit in the lives of one's hearers. It does not matter at all if the audience is not delighted by elegant language and ingenious intonations. The goal of the preacher should be simply to enlighten his hearers and to inspire them to do something about their eternal salvation.[19]

This goal applies both to preaching in an urban setting, where the simple and the learned come together to form a mixed audience and in the country villages, where an illiterate, rustic audience often gathers. In the latter instance, however, the preacher must make a special effort "...to adopt the most popular and lowest kind of eloquence, in order to accommodate his instruction to their weak understanding."[20] To do so, the preacher must put himself in their place and try to imagine himself to be one of them. He should not only adopt a simple style, but also choose subjects that are easy to grasp and understand.[21] His goal should be to explain simply and without embellishment the eternal truths of salvation.

When speaking to the uninstructed, the preacher should also raise questions every so often and supply answers to them. He should use examples from the lives of the saints as well as accounts of punishments inflicted on sinners to serve as negative examples. Above all, it is important for him to speak about practical things related to the quest for holiness and to repeat these insights many times so that they might be impressed more deeply on the minds of the poor.[22]

These key points of Muratori's *Popular Eloquence* offer supporting evidence for Alphonsus's own thoughts on preaching. Together with his own reflections in the earlier part of the instruction, they embody what are, for Alphonsus, the essential traits of authentic Christian preaching.

OBSERVATIONS

When carefully considered, Alphonsus's teaching has great relevance even for today's preachers. The following comments highlight some of the key ideas in Alphonsus's presentation that those entrusted with this important ministry today should listen to carefully and take to heart.

1. A good preacher, for Alphonsus, must be willing to study. He must not wear his learning on his sleeve, however, simply for others to admire and esteem. His learning should be so deep that he does not feel the need to show it off. He must put his learning to the service of God's people by finding new and meaningful ways of making the Gospel message relevant to their lives.

2. Actions, however, speak louder than words. Alphonsus is quick to point out that the preacher's words will not be taken seriously if he does not live an exemplary life. The ministry of preaching is intimately bound up with the spiritual and moral life of the preacher. If his hearers detect a gap between his words and actions, the preacher will soon lose his credibility among his listeners and they will respond by turning their attention elsewhere.

3. The goal of good preaching is the conversion of one's listeners. True conversion takes place in the heart and has concrete effects in a person's thoughts and actions. It is brought about not by the preacher's words, but by the movement of God's grace deep within a person's heart. The preacher's role is to ready a person's heart for the reception of God's grace. He must do so for the glory of God alone and not look for or expect any worldly recompense.

4. In order to be an instrument of conversion, Alphonsus urges the preacher to speak from the heart. The content of a homily or sermon will touch its listeners only if it has first touched the heart of the speaker. For this reason, the material

must be made thoroughly one's own. In order to move others toward God, a preacher must truly feel and practice what he preaches. The homily or sermon will not be effective if he does not speak from his own experience and use it as a way of opening up the Gospel message.

5. For this reason, the homily or sermon must also be rooted in prayer. By this, Alphonsus does not merely mean that the preacher must be a man of prayer (which goes without saying), but that he take the time to pray over the material he is preparing and for those who will hear it. The preacher must bring his ministry of preaching to the Lord. He must ask the Lord for guidance. He must do so while preparing the sermon, while delivering, and even after it as he reflects on its impact.

6. Alphonsus also wants the preacher to use simple, popular language. The pulpit should not be used in order to display one's learning or to receive the praises of others, but as a way of drawing others to God. The preacher should try to speak in such a way so that everyone present will be able to understand what he is saying and be able to remember it. For this reason, he encourages frequent repetition, as well as the use of stories and examples from the lives of the saints.

7. The preacher, for Alphonsus, must also be very practical. He must look for concrete ways of helping his hearers deepen their relationship to the Lord. Very often this will entail explaining concrete devotions and practices that they can use during the day to talk to God. The preacher's duty is to help his hearers deepen their faith in God and to help them to conform their lives to Christ. The goal of the homily or sermon should be to help them to make some concrete and practical resolution to reform their lives.

8. Because conversion is continuous and ongoing, the preacher must help and encourage his hearers to examine their lives so that they know their needs and understand how they can improve. Since a person's deepest need is his or her need for God and since that need is met when a person opens his or her heart to God in prayer, the preacher should use the time at his disposal

to teach his listeners about the way of conversing intimately and familiarly with God. Alphonsus, the doctor of prayer, never tired of emphasizing the importance of preaching about prayer.

9. It is also no mistake that Alphonsus develops his teaching on preaching in an instruction that later, in the second part, focuses on the administration of the sacrament of penance. Preaching is about ongoing conversion; the sacrament of reconciliation is the ordinary means of ongoing conversion in the Church. When people recognize their need for God, they also get in touch with their need to confess their sins. For Alphonsus, the preacher must direct his hearers toward the confessional, and should probably lead the way.

10. Finally, Alphonsus was a master of both spirituality and moral theology. A good preacher must strive to be the same. He should speak about the pressing spiritual and moral issues that his hearers face in their daily lives. He should not be afraid to face such issues. It is, in fact, his responsibility to do so. Preaching is a prophetic ministry. A good preacher will be able to rise to the occasion and, after much prayer and study, will strive to say not what his people want to hear, but what they need to hear. As a prophet, he must know how to challenge and when to console, and the proper time for each.

These ten observations can be used as a simple list of guidelines to determine if a preacher stands within the traditional Alphonsian approach to preaching. While in no way exhaustive, they provide a good sense of how Alphonsus understood this important ministry within the Church and how he should implement it.

CONCLUSION

Alphonsus's teaching on preaching touches the very core of the apostolic life. He considers it a sacred obligation, one that must be carefully prepared for and carried out. If it is not, then the flock will be left untended and the preacher will have much for which he must answer. Good preaching helps both to spread the Gospel and preserve it. It brings others closer to God and contributes to the sanctification of the world. "Faith comes from what is heard," the apostle Paul tells us (Romans 10:17). Alphonsus most willingly and readily concurs.[23]

The good preacher, for Alphonsus, does not draw attention to himself. He speaks to his listeners of God for the glory of God. He does so simply and sincerely as one heart speaks to another. His goal is always to help people along the way of holiness. Doing so means exhorting them to turn away from their sins and to rely completely on the love and mercy of God. It also means teaching them about the ways of prayer and the frequent reception of the sacraments.

Above all, the preacher himself must be a man of prayer. Before the Word of God can touch a congregation's heart, it must first touch the heart of the preacher. This can happen only if the preacher opens his heart and listens to the Word of God, speaking to him in the depths of his soul. A homily or a sermon that does not flow from the heart of prayer will fail to touch people's hearts and have little effect in their lives. Nor will it have any concrete effect in the life of the preacher. Alphonsus offers this teaching on preaching as a way of helping priests to discover the place of God's Word in their lives. If they treasure that Word and take it to heart, their listeners will take their words to heart as well and respond accordingly.

Reflection Questions

1. Do you feel called to the ministry of preaching? Do you enjoy it? Are you good at it? Do you prepare well for the homilies and sermons you give? Is your preaching well received? Is your preaching continuous with the way you live your life? Is there a gap between the two? Do you preach in order to draw attention to yourself or to God? Which of these motivations prevails in your preaching? Are your intentions in any way mixed? Do you try to narrow the gap between what you preach and the way you live your life?

What can you do to focus your efforts more profoundly on bringing others closer to God?

2. When you preach, do you seek to touch the mind or the heart? Which is more important? Is it possible to go to extremes on either end? Is it best to seek a mixture of both when you preach? If so, would you try to emphasize one over the other? Do you see the value of developing different styles of preaching so that you could accommodate your message to different groups and/or personalities? Is it possible to speak to the heart without speaking to the mind?
3. How practical should a homily or a sermon be? Is it possible for the preacher to go too far? Can the preacher intrude in the lives of his listeners without being of any real help to them? How does one keep the proper balance between inspiring one's listeners and offering them concrete practical suggestions for living out their faith? How specific should the preacher's moral exhortations be? Under what circumstances should a preacher encourage a concrete course of action rather than merely providing general moral guidelines?
4. What is the relationship between preaching and sacramental reconciliation? Should preachers speak about sin only in the context of God's willingness to forgive? Once a person's heart is moved and the desire to draw closer to God is aroused, should the preacher offer his listeners specific suggestions to help them to take advantage of the grace they have received? Could they fail to respond to that grace, if nothing is offered to them?
5. Is it important for the preacher to offer a message of hope? What would such a message look like today? What elements would it include? Would the last or eternal things (that is, death, judgment, heaven, hell) enter into such a message? If so, how? Which of these elements would you emphasize in such a message? Which would you deemphasize or leave out altogether? What role does God's mercy and forgiveness have in a message of hope? To what extent must the preacher himself be a person of hope, and forgiveness?

Chapter Four

PREPARING A SERMON

Oh, would to God that there were banished from the church such a vain mode of preaching! It is certain that if all preachers spoke in a simple and in an apostolic manner one would see the world changed.

ALPHONSUS DE LIGUORI, *EXERCISES OF THE MISSIONS*

Alphonsus offers not only practical guidelines but also concrete advice about how preachers should go about preparing their talks. Shortly after the publication of the *Selva*, he published a work entitled, *The Exercises of the Missions* (1760).[1] He dedicates this book entirely to the ministry of preaching and offers an extensive treatment of nearly every aspect of the Redemptorist mission. In chapter seven, he describes in detail the process preachers should go through when preparing a sermon. These suggestions were of great help to Redemptorist missionaries of his day and beyond. With some adaptations, they can benefit all preachers in their attempt to break open the bread of God's Word and share it with their listeners.

SOME IMPORTANT BACKGROUND

Before looking at what Alphonsus actually says about the composition and delivery of the "great sermon" (as he calls it), it would be helpful to examine the contents of the work of which it forms a part. He divides the book into an introduction, twelve chapters, and an appendix. The introduction sets the theme, the chapters examine each major part of the mission, and the appendix looks at other practices necessary for the mission's success. Alphonsus is keenly aware that the content and format of a particular mission must be adapted to the circumstances in which it unfolds. He presents a format that has proved successful for missions preached by him and his Redemptorist confreres in and around the kingdom of Naples. He does not insist on applying this format everywhere in exactly the same way. Missionaries must employ those means that best foster the conversion of hearts in the cultural context in which they find themselves. Otherwise, their pastoral strategies will be ineffectual and fall far short of their stated goals.

In his introduction,[2] Alphonsus begins by reviewing an objection often raised against having missions. For some, a mission does more harm than good, since many quickly go back to sinful patterns of behavior soon after it ends. Such critics, Alphonsus asserts, have no knowledge of the great good accomplished by missions. Even though some relapse into former sins, many receive the grace of conversion and persevere in the state of grace until death. In small country villages, moreover, people receive the opportunity to confess their sins without the fear of being recognized by local confessors.

Alphonsus also acknowledges his debt to the work, *The Missionary Instructed*, by Father Philip de Mura. He condenses the material in this work and sets forth the rules and examples typically used by Redemptorist missionaries. He also adds some of his own reflections from his own experience of thirty-four years of mission preaching. He says he intends the work not just for Redemptorists, but for all priests involved in giving missions; he hopes its plain and concise style will help them in their apostolate. The work, moreover, is full of useful suggestions for sermons written in a familiar style proper to mission preaching.

The chapters themselves cover a wide variety of topics pertinent to missions.[3] Alphonsus classifies them according to exhortations (chapter one), the recitation of the rosary (chapter two), preparing children for confession (chapter three), soliloquies for holy communion (chapter four), teaching Christian doctrine to children (chapter five), instructions for adults (chapter six), the great sermon (chapter seven), other exercises taking place on the mission (chapter eight), devotional exercises recommended for after the mission (chapter nine), general remarks about the giving of missions (chapter ten), the duties of the superior of the mission (chapter eleven), and the virtues that missionaries should practice while giving missions (chapter twelve). These chapters deal with not only the exercises taking place during and after a mission (for example, catechetical instruction, preaching, devotional exercises), but also the responsibilities of the missionaries themselves (for example, the duties of the superior, the virtues the missionaries must practice). Alphonsus is keenly aware that the external success of the mission depends on the interior dispositions of those giving it. If the missionaries themselves are not prayerful men dedicated to the practice of the love of Jesus Christ, their words will have little (if any) effect on their listeners.

Alphonsus concludes with an appendix listing five points of instruction necessary for a successful mission.[4] These include: (1) love for Jesus crucified; (2) devotion to the Mother of God; (3) the necessity of prayer for salvation; (4) flight from dangerous occasions; and (5) the ruin of those who through shame omit to confess their sins. He insists that the mission must address these themes if it is to bear fruit. He presents them in a plain, familiar style and ties them strongly to his emphasis on worldly detachment (*distacco*) and union with God (*unione*).

THE GREAT SERMON

In chapter seven,[5] Alphonsus develops in detail the process involved in composing a mission sermon. He divides the chapter into eight parts, the most important of which are the first three having to do with (1) the invention, (2) the disposition, and (3) the elocution of the sermon.

1. *The Invention.*[6] By "Invention," Alphonsus means the choice of materials for composing a sermon. He considers it a great error for preachers to begin writing their sermons before they have collected the necessary content pertinent to their subject matter. Preachers must gather various texts of Scriptures, arguments, and comparisons before even beginning to think about putting pen to paper. He cites a number of reference collections for finding such materials. After outlining the general classification of materials for the writing of public discourses, he develops in detail those sources known as "Common Topics" (*Loci Communes*).

These sources, Alphonsus maintains, are necessary for the composition of all sermons. They are divided into "intrinsic" (for example, definition, etymology, resemblance, cause) and "extrinsic" (for example, Scripture, Church tradition, the Church Fathers, scholastic theology) topics. Taken together, there are fifteen intrinsic and six extrinsic topics. Although it is not necessary to enumerate the list in its entirety, it bears noting that, for Alphonsus, a good missionary will make use of both types of material. Preachers, in other words, must make balanced use of internal and external material pertaining to the subject. In a sermon on the love of God, for instance, they must tell their listeners about the meaning and origin of love, but also offer examples of its expression for the Scriptures and the tradition of the Church. The etymology of the word *love*, moreover, would be an example of something intrinsic to the topic, while the teachings of the Fathers of the Church would be extrinsic. He concludes this section of the chapter with some concrete advice about the actual practice of gathering materials for a sermon.

2. *The Disposition.*[7] Once they gather appropriate material, preachers must organize their sources in line with the sermon's literary form. In keeping with his emphasis on simplicity of language and style, Alphonsus simplifies the rules of rhetoric for mission preachers. He states that a sermon typically contains three essential parts: the introduction (or *exordium*), the proof, and the conclusion (or peroration).

As far as the introduction is concerned, he lists the various ways in which preachers can begin a sermon and focuses on three principal elements: a general proposition, a connection, and a particular proposition. He gives the following example: "We must be saved; for if we are not saved, we shall be damned; there is no middle way" (general proposition). "Now in order to be saved we must die a good death by leaving the world in the grace of God" (connection). "But it is difficult to die a good death when we have lived a bad life, etc."(particular proposition).[8] The particular proposition can also be divided into its principal points. These points should be restricted in number and announced in a few words. Alphonsus points out, moreover, that "[i]t is *not* a defect...to restrict a sermon to the simple demonstration of the particular proposition without making any division of points."[9]

The proof, for Alphonsus, contains three elements: the introduction, the proof itself, and the refutation. The introduction is a preamble that enters into the proof. Alphonsus lists the various ways the preacher can accomplish this transition.[10] The proof is of an exposition of the principal that should be the body of the sermon. It should be well ordered with the view toward persuading its hearers. Alphonsus asserts that it is best to present only a few of the most convincing proofs rather than amassing a large number that are not developed well and are of little value. After listing the various kinds of argumentation that the preacher can employ in his sermon (for example, syllogisms, examples, inductions), he suggests varying the forms of reasoning for the purpose of effect on the audience. Preachers should list their arguments, moreover, by beginning with solid reasons, then placing the weaker arguments in the middle position, and concluding with those that are most decisive. He also states that preachers ordinarily should begin by presenting those reasons that carry conviction, continue with those that amplify the subject, and conclude with those that touch the heart. Transitions from one point to another should be natural and seek to preserve the unity of the sermon. He supplies numerous examples of how to make such transitions and amplify the subject matter. The proof concludes with the refutation of possible objections.

The conclusion consists of an epilogue, a moral application, and an exhortation. The epilogue, for Alphonsus, should be a brief summary of the sermon that contains its most convincing reasons in a way that already will begin to move the hearts of those present. In the moral application, preachers must be careful not to embarrass particular individuals in the correction of faults and vices. Otherwise, becoming publicly embarrassed, these individuals might harbor ill will toward preachers and remain obstinate to change. Besides the correction of faults, he tells preachers also to suggest remedies that could help the hearers to correct themselves and persevere in good conduct. Preachers should repeat these remedies many times in the sermon so that the poor and uneducated will be able to remember them. The exhortation is one of the most important and most necessary parts of the sermon. The preachers' goal here is to move the hearts of their hearers. To do so, they must humbly ask God for help, for true compunction comes only through the movement of divine grace. Preachers can cooperate with this grace by studying the ways of moving the heart and of regulating the passions. Alphonsus assists preachers in this regard by describing the various passions and warns them not to make their conclusions too long.

3. *The Elocution.*[11] A discussion follows about the various ways in which preachers can use the sermon to convince the understanding and determine the will of their hearers. Elocution, as rhetoricians refer to this art, requires elegance, composition, and dignity.

"Elegance," for Alphonsus, "consists in expressing the idea that one has conceived, and then in making the hearers seize it with the same vividness with which it has been conceived."[12] Seeking clarity and the proper use of words, it avoids terms that are newly coined, antiquated, affected, or vulgar. "Composition," he states, "is the harmony of the discourse which is obtained from the good arrangement of periods [that is, complex sentences] and from their number expressed in suitable words."[13] "The Dignity of elocution," in turn, "...results from the use of tropes and of figures."[14]

Alphonsus uses this section of the chapter to emphasize the importance of avoiding a complex, florid style. Preachers should compose their sermons in a familiar style by employing simple language that everyone can understand and syntax that all can follow. He concludes this part of the chapter with an extensive list of tropes and figures that can be useful in composing a sermon. Tropes, he says, differ from figures in that they give words a sense other than their natural meaning.[15] Preachers must be familiar with these tools of rhetoric and use them effectively to get their message across. However, they should not be used out of vanity or merely to display one's talent.

In the remainder of the chapter,[16] Alphonsus treats such subjects as memory, pronunciation, and gesture (part four). He also gives special instructions for mission sermons (part five), for encouraging the exercises of the devout life (part six), on what should take place during the final sermon of a mission (part seven), and other remarks regarding the sermon (part eight). These five sections are of lesser significance than those on invention, disposition, and elocution. Alphonsus includes them to round out his teaching and to offer important suggestions on the proper delivery of the sermon and on special topics to be included in mission sermons.

OBSERVATIONS

Although Alphonsus focuses chapter seven specifically on the composition and presentation of mission sermons, much of what he says has important implications for other types of preaching. The following remarks draw out these general implications and make appropriate adaptations for today's preachers.

1. When preparing a homily or sermon, preachers should take the trouble to gather material relating to the theme or passage from Scripture under consideration. To do so, they need easy access to a good set of reference materials that represents both the best of the tradition and the latest research on the topic. Preachers should be encouraged to maintain a personal library with key source materials that will help them to break open the bread of God's Word. It would also be helpful if they had access to a theological library that they could consult as the need arises. In gathering material for a homily or sermon, preachers should look for material that speaks to human experience and is both internal and external to the subject matter under consideration. They should order their material well, dividing it into appropriate categories, and strive to find a balance between arguments that make sense in the light of natural reason and those whose authority comes from Scripture and Church tradition.

2. When writing a homily or sermon, preachers should employ a simple structure. It should include a brief introduction, the body or middle part, and a conclusion. In the introduction, preachers should draw from human experience to make contact with their listeners. That example should lead into the body of their discourse, where they will develop their main points. These should be well thought-out and organized. The logic of the preachers' arguments should be clear and easily understandable. The language they use should be simple and to the point. Preachers should tighten loose ends and make sure that one thought flows into the next. They should also be familiar with the art of rhetoric and be able to use the various modes

of persuasion and argumentation to their advantage. They should conclude their discourse in an appropriate manner, making sure that they are appealing not just to the mind, but also to the heart.

3. When delivering a homily or sermon, preachers should avoid complex language and sentence structures. They must seek clarity of speech and expression, using language appropriate both to the occasion and to their listeners. They should avoid showing off their rhetorical skills and drawing attention to themselves in the process. The simplicity of the Gospel message should be matched by the simplicity of their preaching style. They must remember that the success of their discourse is determined not by the sound of their words or the complexity of their arguments, but by the change of heart they bring about in their listeners. For this reason, preachers should always invite their listeners to make concrete changes in their lives. The goal of a homily or a sermon is not to heap admiration and praise upon preachers, but to inspire a person to fundamental conversion.

4. Preachers must also be conscious of the various other skills that go into delivering a successful homily or sermon. Their pronunciation should be clear and their intonations lively yet not affected. They should use gestures appropriate to the occasion, being careful not to gesticulate carelessly or in an exaggerated manner. They should place their voices and body language at the service of the Gospel, using them to express rather than obscure the meaning of the message they are seeking to convey. They should also know when to pause at appropriate moments so that even silence will have an effect on their listeners. The goal of preachers is to break open the bread of God's Word and to share it with their hearers. They should use everything at their disposal to make this happen: mind, heart, spirit, voice, bodily gestures. To do so effectively, they themselves must be thoroughly nourished by God's Word.

5. For this reason, preachers should look upon prayer as something intimately connected to their ministry of preaching. They should ask the Lord to guide them as they gather and

organize their materials. They should also pray over the Scripture passage to which they will be referring and seek to discover its relevance for their own lives. They should ask the Lord to help them as they deliver their homilies and sermons, and they should pray for their listeners, asking the Lord to open their hearts to the message they will hear. Prayer should be one of the central activities of their lives. If they do not pray in this manner, their preaching will be more about themselves than the Gospel message. As a result, their words will fail to convert the minds and the hearts of their listeners. Prayer and preaching go hand in hand. Through prayer, preachers invite the Spirit of God to accompany them as they seek to break open God's Word and share it with their hearers.

These observations remind us of the relevance of Alphonsus's teaching for today. They ask preachers to take ownership of their responsibilities as ministers of God's Word and to do all in their power to cooperate with the grace of the Spirit as they research, compose, and deliver God's message of plentiful redemption.

CONCLUSION

In chapter seven of *The Exercises of the Missions*, Alphonsus goes through the steps of sermon preparation in fine detail. He addresses his remarks not merely to Redemptorist missionaries, but to all who engage in mission preaching. Although he borrows heavily from other sources, he makes a significant contribution to the theory of sermon preparation by simplifying the process so preachers can present the Gospel message in as simple and straightforward a manner as possible.

Alphonsus takes great pains to help preachers act responsibly at every moment of the process. Preachers must know how to gather, organize, and put together their material in a clear, simple, yet elegant style. They must also know how to convince their hearers intellectually, touch their hearts, and move them to action. They must anticipate, moreover, the proper intonations, pauses, and bodily gestures that will be most effective in communicating the Gospel message to their listeners.

Although conditioned by its time, much of Alphonsus's teaching can be adapted to today's circumstances. His call for sound research, good organization, simple language, clarity of style, and dynamic vocal and bodily expression should remind preachers today of both the scope of their task and the great effort needed for effective preaching. His focus on prayer and his insistence on addressing both mind and heart with a view toward orienting one's hearers to concrete action also has a great deal to offer. Today's preachers would do well to take the essential elements of Alphonsus's teaching to heart. Doing so will almost certainly make a difference in the effectiveness of their preaching and in their own response to the call of discipleship.

Reflection Questions

1. How do you go about preparing for a homily or sermon? Do you reflect on the Scripture readings? Do you do so alone or with others? Do you take the time to gather relevant materials from both the tradition and recent research? Do you have access to key resources? Do you organize your material well? Do you allow room for spontaneity and the inspirations of the Spirit?
2. How do you go about actually composing your homilies or sermons? What kind of structure do you give them? Do you draw up an outline or write them down? Do you make sure that your homilies and sermons are easy to follow and understand? Do you use appropriate stories and examples to keep your listeners' attention? Do you edit your material? What can you do to improve your method of composition?
3. What kind of language do you use in your homilies and sermons? Is it simple and easy to understand? Do you try to use words that will communicate the message? Do you use words that evoke images and feelings rather than intellectual abstractions? Is your sentence structure too complicated

for the spoken word? Are you skilled in the art of persuasion? How can this art be used in the proclamation of the Gospel? Can it ever get in the way?

4. How would you describe the way you deliver your homilies or sermons? Do you practice your delivery? Do you go over key words or phrases? Do you practice the intonations and rhythms in your speech? Are you aware of the gestures and bodily expressions that you make? Do you look for feedback from others about the content and delivery of your preaching? Are you able to determine when your delivery is effective.
5. How would you describe the relationship between your spiritual life and your ministry of preaching? Do they merely coexist or are they intimately related? Would you consider your ministry of preaching an extension of your spirituality? If so, in what way? What is the relationship between the ministry of preaching and Redemptorist spirituality? How do they relate to the life of prayer and to Alphonsus's call to preach the Gospel to the poor and most abandoned?

Chapter Five

DEFENDING HIS APPROACH

...the more purely and nakedly the word of God is preached, the more forcibly it strikes the hearts of the hearers; for, according to the Apostle, it is in itself living and effective; so that it is more piercing than a two-edged sword.

ALPHONSUS DE LIGUORI,
LETTER TO A RELIGIOUS ON THE MANNER OF PREACHING

Alphonsus had to defend his approach to preaching before his contemporaries. In 1761, he wrote a lengthy letter to a religious to defend his views on preaching that he had laid out in his *Selva* the year before.[1] This person had informed him of some of the criticisms being made of Alphonsus's positions. The most serious of these came from a "distinguished literary character," who said that preaching in a popular style "...was unworthy of the dignity of the pulpit and degrading to the word of God."[2] Alphonsus responded to this accusation with a comprehensive defense of his teaching. With few adaptations, the points he makes in this letter have relevance for today's preachers as they seek to break open the bread of God's Word for their listeners.

ALPHONSUS'S AIM

Before going into the content of the letter, however, it might be helpful to look at its importance for Alphonsus. Its considerable length and comprehensive nature indicate that he wrote it not merely for the benefit of its intended recipient, but for a wider audience. We know for a fact that, in addition to the religious he addresses, he also sent it to the general superiors of a number of religious orders, all of whom were very impressed with his zealous efforts "...to induce preachers to preach Jesus Christ and not to preach themselves."[3] He also sent it to a great number of bishops with the following note attached:

> I feel great pain when I see so many poor ignorant people who listen to sermons, but derive very little fruit therefrom; and this because of preachers who use an elevated and a florid style, and disdain to lower themselves to break to them the bread of the divine word. It is this that has determined me to publish the present letter, which I have the honor to send your Lordships. I beg you to read it and to have it afterwards read by the priests of the diocese who are engaged in preaching. I would also ask you to send it to the convents of religious priests, and to recommend it to the Superiors to have it read by those that preach. You would also do me a favor if you asked those to read the letter who come to preach the sermons during Advent and during Lent. It is true that the latter bring with them their sermons prepared; but who knows whether by reading it they would not correct themselves in the future, and think of the great account that those preachers will have to render to God who do not make themselves understood by poor ignorant people.[4]

Alphonsus wants his letter read by as many preachers as possible. He sends it to bishops in the hope that they will send it as highly recommended reading to all the preachers of their dioceses. He emphasizes the responsibility of preachers to make themselves understood even to the poor and unlettered. He also reminds them of the account they must give to God for their actions.

Alphonsus wrote his letter not only to defend his teaching but also to uphold the rights of the people in the pew. It caused him great pain to see so many poor, ignorant people listening to sermons, but getting little or no benefit from them. The preacher has a sacred duty to break open the bread of the divine Word. To do so, he must speak in a way that everyone present can understand. Those who employ an elaborate and lofty style do not draw attention to Jesus Christ, but only to themselves. They consider it beneath their dignity to descend to the level of the people and present the good news in a simple, uncluttered style.

In the letter, Alphonsus offers a general instruction on preaching. He gives basic guidelines that should inform all sermons, regardless of their audience, content, or literary type. He wants every preacher to hear his impassioned plea for simplicity of speech and clarity of style. The saints preached in this way to great effect. In his mind, every preacher should be inspired by their example and seek to do the same.

Alphonsus's Defense

In his letter, Alphonsus has to answer not only his critics but also those who find their arguments reasonable. Using all the tools of rhetoric to his advantage, he seeks to sway his reader to his side. We do not have to read very far before witnessing at firsthand Alphonsus's skill at sacred eloquence. He recognizes the need for the art of persuasion in public discourse and uses it exceptionally well. The difference between his use of rhetoric, however, and that of his critics is one of intention. His critics use rhetoric to demonstrate their talent and to bring delight to their audience; he uses it only to draw others closer to Christ.

Alphonsus admits his surprise at his reader's sympathy with

the criticism leveled against him. The heart of the complaint comes when the preacher faces an audience of mixed social and educational backgrounds.

> The objections of my critic, you say, appear somewhat reasonable to you, because a sermon should have all the properties of a discourse, and it is admitted that one of the most essential is to delight the audience; and therefore, when the audience consists both of the ignorant and the learned, the sacred orator should not, by a low popular style, disgust the latter, who are the respectable part of his hearers, but should speak in a manner calculated to please and delight them.[5]

To explain his own beliefs and to answer this and other objections against them, Alphonsus begins by restating much that he already has presented in the *Selva*.

The letter does much more, however, than merely restate the main insights from a previous work. Valuable as it is, what Alphonsus wrote in the *Selva* is a relatively brief presentation of his thoughts on preaching included in a much larger work on the dignity and duties of the priesthood. It forms only half of a single instruction out of the eleven instructions found in the second part. The letter, by way of contrast, is dedicated in its entirety to the topic of preaching. Because Alphonsus is responding to objections made against his approach, moreover, he presents a fully developed thesis carefully designed to answer his critics at every point. If the *Selva* gives Alphonsus's readers the main outline of his approach to preaching, then his letter offers a full-blown comprehensive presentation and defense of his position.

Alphonsus states his thesis very clearly: "My proposition is that, when the audience is composed of the learned and of ignorant, the style of the sermon...should be simple and popular."[6] He backs his statement up with appropriate references from Scripture and the Fathers of the Church. He also refers extensively to the writings of Louis Muratori, one of the most reputable and highly regarded literary figures of his day. Alphonsus cites such sources to show that the wisdom of both the Church and the present age corroborate his claim. His primary answer to his critics is that he has the tradition of the Church and the insights of the finest minds of the day on his side. Who can argue with the like of Saint Paul, Saint Basil, Saint Augustine, Saint Thomas, and Saint Philip Neri, let alone such other noteworthy figures as the learned Marquis Orsi, Father Segneri, Louis of Grenada, and Father John d'Avila?

In making his argument, Alphonsus defines what he means by simple and popular language. "The preacher," he states, "should avoid two things: loftiness of thought and superfluous elegance of language."[7] With regard to lofty thoughts, he borrows an insight from Saint Bonaventure to make his point: "...the bread of the divine word is not to be divided in a manner calculated to indulge curiosity, but must be broken in small pieces on which the little ones may feast."[8] With regard to lofty style, he quotes directly from Saint Paul: "When I came to you, brothers and sisters, I did not come proclaiming the mystery of God to you in lofty words of wisdom. For I decided to know nothing among you except Jesus Christ, and him crucified" (1 Corinthians 2:1–2).[9] A simple style means that to convey his message the preacher will use a straightforward sentence structure and words that are in common use. Preachers should not heap affected and flowery ornaments upon their sermons. In Alphonsus's mind, "...the more purely and nakedly the word of God is preached, the more forcibly it strikes the heart of the hearers."[10] To back up his claims, he refers to a host of authorities who are of the opinion that preachers should use language that will express their meaning simply and serve to persuade their hearers. The rules of rhetoric, he maintains, are necessary for effective preaching. They should not run against the grain of normal conversation, however, but reinforce it. While vulgarity has no place in the sermon, the preacher must be able to communicate his thought in the common language of his audience.

The rules of simplicity and clarity apply to all kinds of preaching and must not be compromised.

Alphonsus does not mean to judge those who preach using a polished, florid style; he only wishes to point out that the saints did not preach that way. He exhorts preachers to follow the example of these "friends of God," who preached for one purpose only: to bring people closer to Christ. Much of the letter is devoted to citing quotations from the saints and examples from their lives about their manner and style of preaching. Saint Thomas Aquinas, Saint Vincent Ferrer, Saint Ignatius Loyola, Saint Francis de Sales, Saint Vincent de Paul, and Saint Francis Regis are just a few of those he refers to in order to back up his case. Preachers, Alphonsus insists, should follow the example of the saints by preaching simply and clearly in order lead others to Christ. If they choose to preach themselves instead by selecting an elevated style far above the capacity of their hearers, they will have much to answer for when they meet God face to face.

Alphonsus then spends a considerable amount of time on the writing of panegyrics, a form of learned discourse that summons an orator's skills of composition and exposition for the purpose of bringing delight to the audience. He laments the lack of fruit and the loss of time caused by such discourses. They would be much more fruitful, he asserts, if "...they were delivered with simplicity, detailing with devout reflection the virtues of the saints."[11] He agrees wholeheartedly with the words of Muratori: "Let a panegyric, if intended to be useful, be composed in that popular and intelligible style of eloquence which instructs and moves the ignorant no less than the learned; but this is oftentimes not understood by him who fancies himself more learned than others."[12] If they do not have this stated purpose in mind, then he would be in favor of doing away with them altogether.

Alphonsus also uses the occasion to address one of the underlying assumptions of his critics: that one of the primary goals of the orator is to entertain. He bases his response on the insights of Saint Francis de Sales who, discouraging the use of worldly eloquence, insists that "[t]he object of the preacher is to convert sinners and to make the just perfect."[13] The preacher, according to Alphonsus, seeks to impart a certain kind of pleasure, but one that is completely different from the aims of secular rhetoric. Once again, he cites the words of Saint Francis de Sales:

> I know that many say the preacher should delight; but as for me, I distinguish, and say, that there is a pleasure consequent on the doctrine which is preached and the impression made upon the hearers; for what soul is so insensible as not to feel extreme pleasure in learning the way to heaven; how to gain Paradise; in comprehending the love which God bears us? And, in order to impart this pleasure, all diligence should be used to instruct and to move. But there is another sort of pleasure which oftentimes is an obstacle to instruction and to persuasion—a tickling of the ear by a profane elegance of language, and a certain balancing of words, which is altogether artificial. And to this, I say without hesitation, that a preacher should not make use of it, because it belongs to profane orators; and whoever preaches in this manner preaches not Christ crucified, but himself.[14]

According to Alphonsus, preachers should seek to please God and no one else. They should speak in an easy and popular style, one that is plain, simple, and unadorned. They should proclaim the truths of the Gospel so that their hearers will turn away from sin, persevere in their faith, and advance in their love for God. He concludes his discourse on preaching by inviting his reader to join him in prayer to Jesus Christ.

OBSERVATIONS

In his letter to a religious, Alphonsus offers a comprehensive presentation and defense of his teaching on the ministry of preaching. He does so with direct and convincing arguments that deepen the insights presented in the *Selva*. The following observations, while in no way exhaustive, concentrate on elements of his teaching having a direct bearing on the ministry of preaching today.

1. *Pastoral.* To begin with, Alphonsus brings a very strong pastoral dimension to his teaching. The goal of the preacher is to draw others closer to God by persuading them to turn away from their sins and to embrace the Lord Jesus Christ. Since faith comes through hearing, he underscores the responsibility of preachers to reach as many people as possible. For this reason, they should present their message so that even the simplest and most uneducated person in the audience will be able to understand it. For him, it makes absolutely no sense whatsoever to tailor one's words only for a select few who would be able to understand and appreciate the complicated thoughts and style associated with worldly eloquence.

2. *Presentation.* Alphonsus, however, does not deny the importance of rhetoric for preaching. He simply wants preachers to use it as a means of drawing others to Christ, rather than as a way of showing off and demonstrating their talents. Preachers should be familiar with the art of rhetoric and use its skills to persuade people to imitate the lives of Christ and his saints. Holiness of life, however, is much more important for the preacher than his ability to persuade. A holy preacher who uses simple, unadorned words in a clear, unadorned style will be much more effective than one whose life does not correspond to the message he proclaims, regardless of its delivery or the quality of its composition.

3. *Use of Time.* The appropriate use of one's time is another reason why Alphonsus is so much against lofty speech and elaborate style. Preachers who write in such a manner can spend

months polishing a single sermon with complicated thoughts and highly stylized sentence structures. When he finally delivers it, however, few (if any) of his hearers will be able to understand what he is saying, let alone bear fruit from the message he is seeking to impart. Such a preacher, according to Alphonsus, fails to make a valuable and efficient use of his time. Rather than using it to compose sermons that will touch the hearts of his audience and move them further along the way of conversion, he simply wastes time composing discourses that display his own talents at the expense of the Gospel.

4. *Pleasure.* Throughout the letter, Alphonsus displays a typically Augustinian understanding of "pleasure." Since God is the only proper object of love, a thing can be truly enjoyed only if it is in some way oriented toward the Divine. The things of the world, therefore, are not to be enjoyed only for themselves, but only to the extent that they lead a person into deeper intimacy with God. When applied to the art of rhetoric, Alphonsus deplores preachers who use it merely for the pleasure it brings to the ears. True rhetoric must lead a person to God. It is not an end in itself, but a tool with which to touch people's hearts and persuade them to turn away from their sins and follow the way of conversion.

5. *Purpose.* For Alphonsus, the preacher must always keep in mind the true purpose of sacred eloquence. The enjoyment a preacher must seek to bring his audience lies not in the sounds of words and polished turns of phrases, but in the experience of God coming from holiness of life. Such an experience comes from God alone. The preacher cannot give it to his hearers, but only lead them to its threshold. True pleasure and enjoyment is a byproduct of the intimacy one shares with God. Rhetoric focusing solely on itself and the skill of the orator is of a purely sensible and transitory nature. Since the pleasure it gives is momentary and passing, it has nothing at all to do with authentic preaching. Preachers who adopt such techniques are fooling themselves and will eventually have much to answer for.

6. *Prayer*. Alphonsus's decision to end his letter with a prayer says much about his understanding of the role of the Spirit in the act of preaching. If faith comes through hearing (Romans 10:17), Alphonsus is also keenly aware that prayer is "the great means of salvation." The effective preacher must be a man of prayer. Only by turning to God himself will the preacher be able to break open the bread of the Word so that the Spirit of the Lord will be able to touch the hearts of his hearers. Like the apostles, their task is "...to show how their spirit manifests the spirit of the divine mysteries so that others might receive the Holy Spirit through them."[15]

7. *Holiness*. In light of the above, Alphonsus is also keenly aware that the ministry of preaching involves walking the way of discipleship. His letter is full of quotations from the saints and examples from their lives. He does so both to strengthen the connection between effective preaching and holiness of life and to underscore the manner in which the saints themselves proclaimed the message of Jesus Christ. For Alphonsus, one of the most telling arguments in favor of preaching in a plain, simple, and unadorned manner is that the saints themselves preached that way. The evidence he puts before his reader is overwhelming. He cites saint after saint on the importance of reaching out to as many people as possible using simple everyday language as a common vehicle of expression. The saints, according to Alphonsus, show us the importance of holiness and simplicity of life. These two values manifested themselves in how they lived and how they preached. He challenges the preachers of his day to do the same.

These observations remind us of the pastoral orientation of Alphonsus's spirituality and his deep desire to place the ministry of preaching at the service of the Gospel call to plentiful redemption. They tell us something of the kind of preaching he thought would be helpful for the Church of his day and remind us of our responsibility to do the same for our own day and age.

Conclusion

In this letter of 1761, Alphonsus offers a comprehensive presentation of the ministry of preaching. In it, he expounds the main elements of his teaching and defends his position against the criticisms that had been leveled against it in the shorter version of it presented a year earlier in his *Selva.*

Although Alphonsus recognizes the need of preachers to incorporate the art of rhetoric in their sermons, he warns them of the danger of using it as an end in itself, merely for the sake of demonstrating their talents and bringing delight to their audience. The purpose of preaching is to draw others closer to God. Preachers who ascend the pulpit using lofty speech and an eloquent style preach themselves rather than Christ and end up doing great damage to the Church's mission.

For this reason, Alphonsus encourages preachers to follow the example of the saints. When breaking open the bread of the Word, he exhorts them to use plain speech and a simple style. In doing so, they will allow the Spirit of the Lord to work through their words to touch the minds and hearts of their hearers. Effective preaching, for Alphonsus, depends not on eloquent words and a lofty style, but on the conviction of one's beliefs that flows from purity of heart and holiness of life. For this reason, preachers must seek to imitate the saints in their quest for holiness. They do so by dedicating themselves to a life of prayer and by seeking to nurture an intimate and vital relationship with the Lord. The saints preached with their lives before they opened their mouths to express the truths of the Gospel. If they wish to be effective, preachers today must strive to do the same. Otherwise, their words will fail to convince and bear precious little fruit.

Reflection Questions

1. What rights do the faithful have with respect to the hearing of God's Word? Have the faithful been informed of these rights? Are they being taught in the seminaries? Do preachers

address them from the pulpit? Do they fulfill their responsibilities by taking the time to break open the Scriptures and share God's Word with the faithful in a simple, easily understandable manner? What about you? Do you connect with the lives of your listeners? Or do you preach at them or use words and ideas that go over their heads?

2. When you preach, do you aim your words at the most educated person in the audience? At the most uneducated? Somewhere in-between? What criteria do you use to shape the content and shape of your message when you find yourself before a mixed, multigenerational group? If it is possible to talk over the heads of your listeners, is it also possible to speak too far below them?
3. How much time do you spend in preparing your homilies and sermons? Too much? Too little? If too much, is it because you are a perfectionist and you are seeking a certain level of content and style that is inappropriate for the audience you typically find yourself facing? If too little, is it because you think the faithful do not really care about what you present to them or because you think that you are so talented that just about anything you give them will be good enough?
4. Do you try to entertain when you preach? If so, how do you do it—through a joke, a story, a play on words? Does it ever get out of hand? When does the desire to entertain interfere with the preaching of God's Word? When does it not? What should you keep foremost in mind when you engage in the ministry of preaching? What traps and snares should you try to avoid?
5. How do you deal with criticism of your preaching? Does it upset you? Do you simply put it out of your mind? Do you listen to it? Do you evaluate it? Do you try to learn from it? How do you respond when you think you have been unfairly criticized? Are you able to defend your approach without being judgmental of those who have spoken up? Has criticism of your preaching ever afforded you the opportunity to deepen your understanding of and approach to the ministry?

Chapter Six

A SERMON BY ALPHONSUS

The Savior of the world, whom, according to the prediction of the prophet Isaiah, men were one day to see on this earth—and all flesh shall see the salvation of God—has already come. We have not only seen him conversing with men, but we have also seen him suffering and dying for the love of us. Let us, then, this morning consider the love which we owe to Jesus Christ at least through gratitude for the love which he bears to us.

ALPHONSUS DE LIGUORI,
SERMON FOR THE FOURTH SUNDAY OF ADVENT

After having examined Alphonsus's teaching on preaching, it might be helpful to look at one of his actual sermons. In this way, we might get a better sense of how he tried to put theory into practice. In 1771, he published a book entitled, *Abridged Sermons for All the Sundays of the Year.*[1] Of the fifty-three sermons in this collection, the one for the Fourth Sunday of Advent is entitled, "The Love of Jesus Christ for Us, and Our Obligations to Love Him."[2] This sermon is a good example of Alphonsus's preaching and warrants careful scrutiny. By looking at how he actually preached, perhaps we can gain better insights into what the Alphonsian charism of preaching might mean for today.

OPENING INSTRUCTIONS

Before going to the sermon, however, we should first look at both Alphonsus's stated aim for the work and the instructions he gives preachers at the beginning. This introductory material provides the context for Alphonsus's sermons and sets the tone for how they are to be used. If we do not pay careful attention to what Alphonsus says here, we may miss some valuable insights into what he hopes to gain by sharing his sermon material with others.

In an opening passage where he offers his purpose for writing the work, Alphonsus states that he is offering "abridged sermons" where the sentiments are expressed briefly, but without becoming vague. He does not want preachers merely to read these sermons from the pulpit or to give them from memory. On the contrary, he seeks merely to provide preachers with material that they will be able to adapt and make their own. For this reason, he says that they can also be used for spiritual reading. Once preachers reflect upon the material and think about its value for their own spiritual life, they will be able to incorporate it into their preaching. At all costs, Alphonsus wishes to avoid having preachers use his sermons as a crutch or as a means of escaping their own responsibilities. "A preacher will scarce ever deliver, with zeal and warmth, sentiments he has not made in some manner his own."[3] Alphonsus also makes reference to the easy and simple style of the sermons and of the abundance of passages from Scripture, the Fathers of the Church, and the saints, most of which could not be used in a single sermon. His aim is to offer his readers an abundance of material for each Sunday of the year that they can expand upon, adapt, and arrange as they see fit. The work, in other words, is meant to be an aid to preaching, rather than a set of ready-made sermons that a preacher can simply dust off and use at will.[4]

Later, in his "Instructions to Preachers," Alphonsus offers his readers a summary of his teaching on preaching that he has presented in earlier works. He presents six fundamental points: (1) the proper end of preaching, (2) the material one should treat, (3) the parts of a sermon, (4) elocution, (5) pronunciation and gesture, and (6) the length of the sermon.

As far as the end of the sermon is concerned, Alphonsus wants preachers to seek nothing else than to bring others to God. For this reason, they should pray fervently to God to inflame their hearts with love. For their topics, preachers should focus on those things that will move their hearers to detest sin and to love God; they should preach often on the last things (death, judgment, hell, heaven and life everlasting), Christ's love for humanity, and the confidence in Mary's intercession. They should emphasize God's love rather than the fear of punishment and focus on practical advice that will enable their hearers to persevere in their vocations. Alphonsus offers a relatively simple sermon structure for preachers to follow (introduction, proof, conclusion). He exhorts preachers to commit their sermons to memory and to employ a simple style of writing, delivery, and gesture. What he suggests for the length of the sermon was considered moderate for his day (one hour during Lent, three quarters of an hour on Sundays, and a half an hour for a parochial instruction).

These "Instructions" demonstrate Alphonsus's concern for preaching and his desire that preachers give their hearts to it. Our analysis of his sermon on the love of Jesus will now show that he also took it completely to heart himself.[5]

Alphonsus's Sermon on the Love of Jesus Christ

As stated earlier, Alphonsus offers this sermon for the Fourth Sunday of Advent. He divides it into three easily distinguishable parts: introduction (or *exordium*), proof, and conclusion (or peroration). Each of these has further component parts that fit together to make the sermon a unified literary whole.

1. The introduction (or *exordium*) usually contains a general proposition, a connection or link, and a particular proposition. It can also contain other introductory and or concluding elements that help the flow of the argument. This particular sermon begins with an introductory verse from Scripture, "and all flesh shall see the salvation of God" (Luke 3:6).[6] The general proposition reads as follows: "The Savior of the world, whom, according to the prediction of the prophet Isaiah, men were one day to see on earth—*and all flesh shall see the salvation of God*—has already come."[7] Then comes the connection with the main theme of the sermon: "We have not only seen him conversing with men, but we have also seen him suffering and dying for the love of us."[8] The conclusion follows: "Let us, then, this morning consider the love which we owe to Jesus Christ at least through gratitude for the love which he bears to us."[9] The introduction then ends with a listing of the main points of the sermon: "In the first point we shall consider the greatness of the love which Jesus Christ has shown to us; and in the second we shall see the greatness of our obligations to love him."[10] In a few short sentences, Alphonsus roots his sermon in Scripture, tells his listeners exactly what it is going to be about, and even gives them a breakdown of its major sections.

2. Alphonsus presents the corpus, or proof, of the sermon in terms of a perfect syllogism—with a major, a minor, and a conclusion—but without making it appear so. The argument Alphonsus makes in the sermon is quite clear: (a) Jesus died in order to show his love for us (major); (b) the cross itself is a convincing proof of God's foolish love for us (minor); and (c) we have an obligation to love him in return (conclusion). Since he is preaching to the faithful about truths of the faith, Alphonsus does not set out to offer a rational proof of his argument.[11] Arguing from within the faith, he employs Scripture, the Church Fathers, and sayings of the saints to amplify each point, sustain his line of reasoning, and thus move the hearts of his audience.

To show that Jesus died out of love for us (the major), Alphonsus quotes from the gospels (Matthew 26:8; John 15:13), the letters of Paul (Ephesians 5:2; Philippians 2:8), and a number of Church Fathers and holy saints (Augustine, John Chrysostom, Francis of Assisi). His basic point is that Jesus did not have to die to redeem humanity: "One drop of his blood would be sufficient for our redemption. Even a prayer offered to his eternal Father would be sufficient; because, on account of his divinity, his prayer would be of infinite value, and would therefore be sufficient for the salvation of the world, and of a thousand worlds."[12] Jesus died not because he had to, but out of love for us: "To show how much he loved us, he wished to shed not only a part of his blood, but the entire of it by dint of torments....What more can one man do for another than give his life for him?"[13]

While still in the first part of his sermon, Alphonsus shifts his focus by telling his listeners that the cross itself is proof of God's love for them (the minor). He tells them this directly: "O Christian! Should a doubt ever enter your mind that Jesus Christ loves you, raise your eyes and look at him hanging on the cross."[14] To support his claim, he once again quotes from the gospels (Matthew 26:26; Luke 12:50; 22:15; John 13:1), the letters of Paul (1 Corinthians 1:23; 2 Corinthians 5:14), the Book of Revelation (1:5) and a number of Church Fathers and holy saints (Ambrose, Gregory the Great, Bernard of Clairvaux, Francis de Sales, Francis of Paul, Thomas of Villanova, and Lawrence Justinian). His basic point is that the cross is a sign of God's foolish and excessive love for us: "Who can believe that a God, most happy in himself, and who stands in need of no one, should take human flesh and die for the love of men, who are his creatures? This would be to believe that a God became foolish for the love of men."[15] Yet this is precisely what Christians believe: "...it is of the faith that the Son of God has shed all his blood for the love of us, to wash away the sins of our souls.... Hence the saints were struck dumb with astonishment at the consideration of the love of Jesus Christ."[16] Alphonsus makes brief mention of the gift of the Eucharist as another sign of God's foolish love for us.

After demonstrating both from Scripture and Tradition that Jesus died on the cross to show his foolish love for us, Alphonsus embarks on the second part of his sermon, where he seeks to show our obligation to love him in return (the conclusion of the syllogism). Alphonsus makes a simple case: "He who loves, wishes to be loved...Jesus Christ came on earth to light up the fire of divine love in the hearts of men."[17] To support his claim, he quotes from the psalms (Psalm 38:4), the gospels (Luke 12:49), the letters of Paul (Romans 14:9; 2 Corinthians 5:15), and the apostles and saints (Andrew, Bernard of Clairvaux, Bonaventure). His basic point is that God requires nothing from us but to be loved. We can accomplish this through prayer: "Meditation is the blessed furnace in which the holy fire of divine love is kindled. Make mental prayer every day, meditate on the passion of Jesus Christ, and doubt not but you too shall burn with this blessed flame."[18] Meditating on the passion face to face with the mystery of the cross enables us to love God with our whole hearts.

3. The conclusion (or peroration) generally contains an epilogue, a moral exhortation, and a passionate appeal. In his epilogue, Alphonsus recommends the practice of meditation: "I conclude, my most beloved brethren, by recommending you henceforth to meditate every day on the Passion of Jesus Christ. I shall be content, if you daily devote to this meditation a quarter of an hour. Let each at least procure a crucifix, let him keep it in his room, and from time to time give a glance at it saying: 'Ah! My Jesus, you have died for me, and I do not love you.'"[19] In his moral exhortation, he tells us that meditation is pleasing to God: "Had a person suffered for a friend injuries, buffets, and prisons, he would be greatly pleased to find that the friend remembered and spoke of him with gratitude. But he should be greatly displeased if the friend for whom these trials had been borne were unwilling to think or hear of his sufferings. The frequent meditation on his Passion is very pleasing to our Redeemer; but the neglect of it greatly provokes his displeasure."[20] In his passionate appeal, he speaks of the consolation that

frequent meditation brings to us, especially at the hour of death: "Oh, how profitable and sweet the meditation of Jesus on the cross! Oh! How happy the death of him who dies in the embraces of Jesus crucified, accepting death with cheerfulness for the love of that God who has died for the love of us!"[21] He also points out how devotion to the passion also increases our devotion to the sorrows of Mary.

Observations

Although it does not do justice to the piece as a whole, the above structural presentation demonstrates how well thought-out and carefully constructed were the sermons of Alphonsus. It also offers an opportunity to make some general remarks about his approach to preaching.

1. To begin with, Alphonsus uses a relatively simple structure for his sermons. Each has a beginning, a middle, and an end. Each of these, in turn, is further divided into three parts. The main part of the sermon is carefully constructed to make one major point which, as in the present instance, he sometimes breaks down further for the sake of clarity. As a popular preacher, Alphonsus was keenly aware of the difference between the written and spoken word. His wrote his sermons down, but with a keen understanding that they would be delivered orally. For this reason, he uses a simple language, structure, and style to drive home a single point. Everything else in the sermon is meant to support that single point. In the present instance, his message is clear. The cross is a sign of God's foolish love for us and we should love him in return.

2. Alphonsus's introduction (*exordium*) and conclusion (peroration) provide carefully crafted bookends for his main argument. They are simply written and go straight to the point. In his introduction, Alphonsus moves from the general to the particular to introduce his listeners to the main topic of the sermon. In the conclusion, he restates the main point of the sermon by offering listeners realistic practices for growth, as well as

sound moral advice, and edifying sentiments. When they are examined in conjunction with the main body of the sermon, it becomes clear that Alphonsus's approach is to tell his listeners what he is going to tell them, tell them, and then to tell them that he told them. Once again, the theme of repetition comes through in his style of preaching, this time in the very structure of the sermon itself.

3. In his opening instructions to preachers at the beginning of the book, Alphonsus says that the body (or proof) of a sermon "...should be a perfect syllogism without appearing so."[22] By this statement, he means that the sermon should be constructed logically, but primarily ordered to persuade one's listeners. A sermon, for Alphonsus, is not an academic lecture. That is to say that its rational line of argumentation should not be the focus of attention, but a part of an underlying framework that allows the preacher to use language and persuasion to move the hearts of his listeners. A sermon, in other words, must be rooted in reason, but constructed and delivered in a way that touches the audience on a deeper level. Good preachers base their sermons on sound arguments, but present them in a way that helps their listeners commit themselves to change.

4. Alphonsus fills his sermons with numerous citations from Scripture, the Church Fathers, and the sayings of the saints. His goal here is to break open God's Word and to share with his listeners the rich treasures of the Church's tradition. In doing so, he wishes to demonstrate that the point he is making is deeply rooted in Catholic belief and practice. Providing a number of such citations in a sermon also serves the rhetorical purpose of driving a point home by repeating it a number of times from a slightly different perspective. As he points out in the opening instructions to his work, Alphonsus leaves the preacher to decide how much a particular point should be amplified in such a manner. Among other things, such a judgment depends on the nature of the sermon, the time allotted for it, and the composition of the audience.

5. Since we have no voice recording or video tape of

Alphonsus delivering this or any other sermon, we can only imagine how he would actually have delivered it. Given the careful way he follows the guidelines for composing a sermon that he offers in his opening instructions to preachers, however, we can assume that his elocution, pronunciation, and gestures were all carefully crafted to contribute positively to the sermon's overall effect. Alphonsus, in other words, most likely practiced what he preached not only regarding the writing of a sermon, but also with respect to its delivery. To move the hearts of his listeners, he made sure that he knew his material so well that he had no need of a text or written prompts. He made sure that he knew the material thoroughly before he presented it to his listeners.

6. Alphonsus's sermons also have a very practical orientation. In the present instance, it is not enough for him to expound on Jesus' love for us and on our obligation to love him in return. He also offers very concrete, practical advice on how we can engage in meditation as a way of deepening our love for him. Alphonsus's spirituality is very much oriented toward practice and his sermons clearly reinforce that quality. It is also important to note that the practices he recommends are realistic. In this sermon, for example, he suggests to his listeners that they meditate on Jesus' passion for fifteen minutes a day and that they buy a crucifix and put it in a prominent place in their rooms so that they will be reminded of Jesus' suffering and death when they look at it. Alphonsus's insistence on providing realistic helps in the spiritual life display a deep pastoral sensitivity to his listener.

7. Finally, it is not surprising that the primary practice offered by Alphonsus to his listeners is that of prayer. He believed that prayer was "the great means of salvation" and that meditation (or "mental prayer" as he often called it) in particular was morally necessary for salvation. One of the reasons why he is known as the "doctor of prayer" is because he emphasized time and again that preachers should drive home to their listeners the importance of prayer as a means of growing in intimacy

with Christ. He preached and wrote about prayer every chance he got and still felt that he had not done near enough. Alphonsus considered prayer essential in sermon preparation. If a preacher does not pray about what he should preach about, then there is a strong likelihood that, in the end, he will wind up preaching himself rather than Christ crucified. Prayer is what keeps a person focused on Christ. For Alphonsus, this was especially true for the preacher of God's Word.

CONCLUSION

The sermon for the Fourth Sunday of Advent, "The Love of Jesus Christ for Us, and Our Obligation to Love Him," is a carefully crafted piece of popular preaching. Alphonsus's expressed aim in this sermon is to inflame the hearts of his listeners to a deep love for Jesus Christ. To achieve this aim, he employs a simple language, structure, and style so that his words might make sense to as many people as possible.

This emphasis on simplicity, however, does not mean that Alphonsus has compromised on the quality of the material he uses for his sermon. Every page of this sermon is steeped in Scripture, the Fathers of the Church, and the sayings of the saints. In doing so, he not only drives his main message home to his listeners but also immerses them in the living tradition of the Church. He presents his listeners with the living voices of the past that join him in proclaiming the love of Jesus Christ and his desire to be loved.

Jesus, according to Alphonsus, "...came on the earth to light up the fire of divine love in the hearts of men."[23] His preaching was an important element of his mission and continues to be so for his followers. Alphonsus wanted Redemptorist missionaries to use God's Word to inflame the hearts of their listeners with divine love. He led them not only by his words but also by example. His sermons offer eloquent testimony of his desire to preach Jesus' message of plentiful redemption. Everything in his life was oriented toward this one all-important end.

Reflection Questions

1. If you had to give a brief presentation on the purpose of preaching, what would you say? What would you emphasize? How would you say it? Do you agree with Alphonsus's description of its purpose? Is there anything you would add? Is there anything you would take away from it?
2. If you had to give a set of instructions to preachers on how to go about composing a homily or sermon, what would you say? What would you say about the structure of the homily or sermon? What would you say about language and style? What would you say about pronunciation, delivery, and gestures? What would you say about the length of time for various types of homilies and sermons?
3. What, in your opinion, are the most important themes upon which to preach? Do you agree with the list offered by Alphonsus? Are there any you would add? Are there any you would take away? How important a topic is prayer? Where does it fit into your list?
4. What role does rational argument play in the composition of a homily or sermon? What role do Scripture and Church tradition play? What role do the lives and sayings of the saints play? Which would you emphasize more? Are there any you would never emphasize?
5. Do you believe that every homily or sermon ought to have a practical orientation? If so, how can this best be accomplished? If not, under what circumstances would you make an exception? What approaches have not been helpful in making the sermon practical? What have you found to work? Can a homily or a sermon ever be too practical?

Chapter Seven

Alphonsian Preaching Today

When the opportune time comes, and the Lord opens the door to them for the preaching of the word (cf. Colossians 4:9), the members are always ready to give witness to the hope that is in them (cf. 1 Peter 3:1). They bring to completion the silent witness of their brotherly presence by preaching the mystery of Christ with confidence and constancy (cf. Acts 4:13. 29, 31). They will never grow weary of invoking the Holy Spirit, so that they may always be able to cooperate more wholeheartedly in bringing the mystery of redemption in Christ to full effect. For the Spirit has command of every situation, puts the appropriate word on the lips of the preacher and opens hearts to receive it.

REDEMPTORIST C&S, GENERAL CONSTITUTION 10

Having examined Alphonsus's teaching, as well as one of his sermons, we are now in a position to say something about what preaching in the Alphonsian tradition might look like today. It would be a mistake to think that we can simply take his approach and apply it without adaptation to our present circumstances. To do so would be insensitive to the spiritual needs and cultural sensitivities of people today. It would be equally mistaken, however, to simply think that Alphonsus has nothing to offer today's Redemptorists as they seek to break open God's Word and share it with the people they serve. Although Alphonsus's approach to preaching was influenced by the cultural milieu in which he lived, it also offers something of universal value for all Redemptorist preachers to ponder and use. The challenge for us today is to distill that value from Alphonsus's teaching and then to make relevant adaptations to our current situation. Our purpose in this chapter is to help Redemptorist preachers begin this process of evaluation and relevant adaptation.

Distilling Basic Principles

We have already seen in earlier chapters that Alphonsus wanted his Redemptorist missionaries to encourage their listeners to holiness and conversion of heart. They were to be deep men of prayer, who broke open the bread of God's Word for others with preaching that was rooted in Scripture, Tradition, and the power of the Spirit. Redemptorist preachers were to draw attention not to themselves, but to Christ. They were to follow Christ's lead by preaching in a simple style and with heartfelt fervor. They were to take their preaching seriously, both as individuals and as a community. They were to be an apostolic community that preached Christ crucified to those with little or no access to the ordinary means of salvation provided by the Church. In preparing their homilies and sermons, they were to make sure that even the simplest, most uneducated person in the church would be able to understand them. Language, style, structure, pronunciation, and gesture were all carefully scrutinized to ensure the most optimal effect.[1]

Preaching, for Alphonsus, was an essential element of the Redemptorist charism. It was at the center of the apostolic life of the Congregation and a part of its very reason for existence.

From the above description of the kind of preachers Alphonsus wanted his missionaries to be, we can also distill a number of basic principles. Five in particular stand out.

1. *A Sense of Urgency*. To begin with, Redemptorists must have a deep sense of urgency about the message they proclaim. They must believe in the good news and feel strongly about their listeners' need to hear it. This sense of urgency must spring from deep within their hearts. It cannot be feigned or contrived, but must stem from a deep desire to serve and from the conviction that no message is more important to the world today than that of God's love for humanity. Redemptorists must view their preaching ministry in terms of a sacred trust of breaking open the bread of God's Word so that it might be a source of nourishment and growth for others. They must consider their preaching central to their lives and mission. They must long to preach the Good News of Jesus Christ and believe that the lives of their listeners can be deeply affected by what they say.

2. *The Necessity of Prayer*. Redemptorists get in touch with this sense of urgency through their personal relationship with Christ. This relationship is nurtured through prayer, especially mental prayer (or meditation), which Alphonsus taught was morally necessary for salvation. Without prayer, a person cannot come to share in the intimate friendship of Christ. Without such a relationship, Redemptorists will lack an authentic experiential basis from which to preach *metanoia,* or fundamental conversion, to those they are seeking to serve. One cannot tell others of the great urgency and importance of friendship with Christ without having first experienced it yourself. When seen in this light, prayer is the pulpit one preaches from and the subtext of every effective homily or sermon. From beginning to end, prayer must permeate every aspect of the preaching process. Without prayer, Redemptorist preachers will simply not be effective. Their words will fail to draw others to Christ.

3. *Thorough Preparation*. To fulfill their responsibilities to God, to their listeners, and to themselves, Redemptorists need to prepare themselves thoroughly for what they are going to

say. To do so, they must gather appropriate material for their homilies or sermons, read this material through, reflect on its significance for their lives and the lives of their listeners, decide on what they want to say, write it down or at least structure it in a simple, easy-to-understand manner, and practice how they intend to express themselves. Every aspect of the discourse should be readied with care. Prayer, moreover, should be the silent companion of the Redemptorist as he readies himself for his ministry. Without such thorough preparation, the preacher denigrates the preaching moment by failing to allow God's Word to take root in his heart and express itself through him with power and conviction. Sloppiness in preparation usually results in sloppy preaching. Why should people listen to someone who has not taken the time to organize his thoughts and deliver them with conviction?

4. *Effective Presentation.* Redemptorists also need to ensure that they deliver their homilies or sermons as effectively as possible. To do so, what they wish to say must be so internalized that their words will flow easily from their tongues in rhythms and tones that facilitate the communication of God's Word. They should also try to use visible expressions and gestures in a way that enhances their message rather than detracts from it. They must make every effort to avoid giving the impression that their words are unduly affected or overly dramatized. They must speak spontaneously and from the heart, but not come across as though they are entertaining or giving a performance. The sound delivery of a homily or sermon will draw people to Christ and lead them along the way of conversion. Before they mount the pulpit, they would do well to pray for their listeners and ask God for help in making the minutes at their disposal as effective a time as possible.

5. *Profound Reflection.* After they have given their homilies and sermons, Redemptorists need to reflect on what they have said and how they have said it. They should do so in a prayerful manner that helps them to evaluate their various words and gestures so that they can share God's Word more effectively

with others. This process of profound reflection is important so that preachers will know their various strengths and weaknesses. It should be done both individually and communally, by the preacher himself and by the other members of community to which he belongs. At appropriate times, it may even be helpful to seek feedback from their listeners. Redemptorists need to know how they come across to those who listen to them. Sound feedback will help them to refine their manner of preaching and enable them to be better servants of God's Word. Redemptorists who fail to reflect upon their preaching will be doomed to repeat the same mistakes that have made their way into their homilies and sermons.

These basic principles highlight the spiritual dimensions of Redemptorist preaching and the intricate process of preparation, presentation, and reflection that must accompany it. If they are to be effective preachers, Redemptorists must allow these to permeate their approach to God's Word and the way they break it open and share it with others. They also must find relevant ways of incorporating these principles into methods that resonate with their traditions and are relevant to the lives of their hearers.

PRACTICAL SUGGESTIONS

A key question for Redemptorists today is how to implement the above principles in relevant and practical ways. The following suggestions are intended as practical guidelines for helping to embody Alphonsus's spirit and teaching in the concrete circumstances of their preaching ministry.

1. To begin with, it is important for Redemptorists to understand what is meant by a "sense of urgency." Such an expression can easily lend itself to exaggeration and unhealthy caricature. Two extremes are to be avoided. On the one hand, we must avoid rushing into things. Good preaching needs time to ripen and mature. Writing a homily or sermon should not be a matter of getting a job done in as short a time as possible, but

of listening to one's heart and pondering what message God's Spirit is revealing there for the good of one's listeners. On the other hand, we must be careful not to allow a heightened sense of the immediacy of divine judgment detract from the overall gospel message of God's mercy, love, and forgiveness. A true sense of urgency steers a middle course between these exaggerated extremes. Above all, we are called upon to highlight the importance of hearing the call to fundamental conversion and change of heart (*metanoia*).

2. Redemptorists should thus understand that the "sense of urgency" flows from the conviction of the radical need of their listeners to hear God's Word and that they are the ones who have been especially selected to pronounce those words. When seen in this light, a "sense of urgency" flows directly from a deep sense of call. If we are to be effective preachers, we need to have a clear sense of identity about who we are and what we are being called to do. We must be made to see that preaching the Word of God is a privilege that carries with it a great responsibility. We need to be thoroughly convinced that the message we preach is the most important thing that God's people need to hear at that particular moment in time. The only way to understand what those words might be is for us to be radically rooted in the Word ourselves so that our hearts will be open to God's Spirit and able to discern the message we are called upon to speak.

3. For Redemptorists to be radically rooted in God's Word, they need to turn constantly to God in prayer. For Alphonsus, the best way for someone to become a person of prayer is to engage in the practice of meditation, or mental prayer, which he claims is morally necessary for salvation. Mental prayer, according to Alphonsus, has a clearly defined beginning, middle, and end, what he calls the preparation, the meditation itself, and the conclusion. In the *preparation*, the person praying affirms his or her faith in God's presence, makes an act of humble contrition, and requests enlightenment during the upcoming exercise. The *meditation* involves four movements: (1) reflecting on

some aspect of the life of faith, (2) raising one's heart and affections to God, (3) asking God for help, and (4) making some practical resolutions to improve one's walk with the Lord. The *conclusion* consists of thanking God for the enlightenment received, affirming one's decision to carry out the resolution, and asking God for the grace of fidelity. Regardless of whether we follow Alphonsus's approach, as Redemptorists, we need to be deep men of prayer who share in the intimacy of the divine. Otherwise, we will have no experiential base from which to share the Good News of Jesus our Redeemer.[2]

4. Alphonsus considers mental prayer essential for growth in the spiritual life: it enlightens our minds; it disposes us to practice the virtues; and it helps us to pray as we ought. Redemptorists can use this prayer form not only as a means of drawing closer to Christ but also as a way of vitalizing their preaching ministry and giving it a deep and authentic sense of urgency. We should be encouraged to bring our preaching to prayer and our prayer to our preaching. Alphonsus's approach to mental prayer offers us a very specific way of doing so. The period of preparation, for example, will encourage us to affirm our faith in Christ, seek mercy and forgiveness for our sins, and look for ongoing guidance from the Lord. The body proper of the meditation will help us to reflect upon the theme we will preach on, get in touch with our feelings about it, take an honest look at our own needs and those of our listeners, and make concrete decisions about how to go about conveying our message. The conclusion will lead us to thank God for the light we have received, seek continued help in our preaching ministry, and humbly ask for the grace of perseverance.

5. Homily or sermon preparation should be both remote and immediate. For Redemptorists today, remote preparation should include courses in homiletics given during seminary training and periodic updating through the reading of homiletic books and journals and continuing education courses. In addition to these important formation activities, we should also have remote preparation for each homily or sermon we deliver. This

includes going over the readings well in advance, praying over them, identifying the material one wishes to emphasize, selecting relevant metaphors and examples that will carry our message, composing our homilies or sermons with simple language and practicing its presentation and clear delivery. As the time for delivering the homily or sermon approaches, the immediate preparation should involve refining the rough points we have encountered in the remote preparation and then turning the entire process and moment of delivery over to the Lord in prayer. The goal in the entire preparation process is for us to internalize God's message in such a way that we are able to speak God's message with power and conviction to those before us.

6. In addition to the remote and immediate preparation, Redemptorists today need to be able to let go of their homilies and sermons so that the Spirit of God can work through them in the present moment. Although he warns inexperienced preachers from doing so, Alphonsus applauds the capacity of the seasoned preachers to speak extemporaneously, without any notes, and seemingly with little preparation beforehand.[3] This ability normally comes from years of preaching experience that gives seasoned preachers a sense of ease and familiarity from the pulpit. Their natural ease in preaching comes from the many homilies or sermons that they have painstakingly worked on and delivered in the past and which are now so deeply internalized that they are able to tap into them at will and even to create innovative nuances while they are actually standing before their hearers. Experienced preachers are so skilled in their craft that they are able to speak spontaneously in the Spirit with words and gestures that move people's hearts and that go to the core of the gospel message.

7. As far as presentation is concerned, Redemptorists today need to remember that all of their preparation—both immediate and remote—culminates in the relatively short time that they are standing before their hearers. The presentation of our homilies and sermons needs to be spontaneous and rooted in the present moment. We need to have our entire beings focused on

our hearers and the way our words and gestures are affecting them. Every dimension of our human makeup—the physical, emotional, intellectual, spiritual, and social—needs to act in harmony as we break open the bread of God's Word for our hearers. For this to happen, we need to be at home with ourselves and with our God. Only then will we be able to invite others to share in the Lord's friendship; only then will we be able to make others feel at home in the fellowship of the communion of saints. As Redemptorists, we need to convey our message to our hearers as though we were unwrapping for them a gift from God. Our words and gestures must seek to express the infinite depths of God's love and his unbounded willingness to forgive.

8. Just how do we preach this message of love and forgiveness? Before anything else, Redemptorists today must first experience it for themselves. We cannot share with others what we ourselves do not possess. We must make sure that we are right with God before we invite others to do so. Once we have reconciled ourselves with the Lord, we must do all in our power to be ourselves before others as we are in our faith. Since every person is unique, each of us will have a slightly different style and way of doing so. We must be ourselves when we preach. We must develop those voice patterns, inflections, intonations, and gestures that bring out our deepest selves. We must stand before our listeners as we stand before God, without any masks or false pretensions. We must speak the truth as we have discerned it in our hearts and reflected upon it for the good of God's people.

9. As far as reflection upon homilies and sermons is concerned, Redemptorists need to develop ways of pondering what they have said and then evaluating its effectiveness. This should be done both individually and in groups (first with other preachers and then with smalls groups of their listeners). Once again, the various levels of human existence must be taken into account: the physical, emotional, intellectual, spiritual, and social. One method of reflection would be for us to adapt

Alphonsus's approach to mental prayer to the needs at hand. That is to say that we can use our preaching experience as the topic of prayer, following the various steps involved in the preparation, meditation, and conclusion as a means of laying open this experience before God and looking at it from a variety of perspectives. This process could be done both individually and adapted to a group context. The strength of this approach would be the way in which it binds the process of reflection so closely to prayer.

10. Finally, when reflecting on their experiences, Redemptorists today should examine the role played by silence in every moment of the process: the preparation, the presentation, and the reflection. God speaks to us through silence. If we are to be effective from the pulpit, we need to be at home in silence. Solitude of heart, as Alphonsus would call it, is necessary for any intimate relationship with God. To reach such a relationship, we must befriend silence and be at home with it. When preaching, we must know when to allow silence to break through our words so that the Spirit of God will be able to show itself to our listeners deep within our hearts. We must reflect upon how we use silence in our words and gestures. We must try to understand how our homilies and sermons allow God to touch the hearts of our listeners. More often than not, this happens not simply through what we say, but through what we do not say, or, better yet, through what the Spirit of God utters in the silent spaces between our words and beneath the breaths that sustains them.

Conclusion

Alphonsus's teaching has much to offer today's Redemptorists. Although it is very much a product of his own day, it contains a number of very basic principles that have deep relevance for the way we should approach this very important ministry of the Church. It reminds us that preachers must be rooted in prayer and possessed of a deep sense of urgency about the importance of the gospel message. It also tells us that they must take time to prepare, present, and reflect upon the various aspects involved in their ministry.

As Redemptorists, we need to find ways of incorporating these basic principles into our preaching ministry. The practical suggestions outlined above should help us become more effective heralds and communicators of God's Word. Because we are unique individuals, however, we must adapt these basic principles and practical suggestions in ways suitable to our own styles and mode of expressions.

Alphonsus was keenly aware that Redemptorist preachers conveyed God's Word primarily with their lives and only secondarily with their words. He insisted on continuity between their words and actions and saw prayer (and mental prayer, in particular) as a primary means of accomplishing this aim. We will be able to practice what we preach only if we nourish a deep intimate relationship with our Lord. If we overlook this fundamental spiritual dimension of our lives, our words will have little, if any, lasting effect in the lives of our listeners.

REFLECTION QUESTIONS

1. Do you believe that preachers need a sense of the urgency of the message? If so, why? If not, why not? Do you yourself have a sense of urgency when you preach? If so, what is it like? How would you describe it? How does it motivate you? How does it affect the way you go about your ministry? If not, would you like to have such a sense? What can you do to get it? What could you do to deepen what sense of urgency you already have?
2. Why is prayer so important for the spiritual life? Why is prayer so important for preaching? Does Alphonsus's approach to mental prayer appeal to you? Have you ever tried it? If so, which steps do you find the easiest? Which do you find the most difficult? Which steps do you find to be most applicable to the preaching process? Why?

3. How do you go about preparing for a homily or a sermon? How would you describe it? Do you go about it competently or irresponsibly? Do you have both remote and immediate preparation? Do you gather relevant materials? Do you reflect and pray over them? Do you write your homilies or sermons down? Do you make an outline of them? Do you practice them? What could you do to improve your preparation?
4. How would you describe the way you deliver a homily or sermon? Are you animated by what you say? Does your manner of presentation depend on the occasion? Does it depend on your state of preparation? On your mood or disposition? Do you engage your listeners? Do you establish a bond with them? Do you preach in the present moment? Do you ever feel as though God is speaking through you? If so, how would you know it to be true? What could you do to improve your presentation and delivery?
5. Do you reflect on your homilies or sermons after giving them? If so, how do you reflect on them? Do you do so alone or with others? Do you reflect on them from a variety of perspectives, taking into account the physical, intellectual, emotional, spiritual, and social dimensions of human existence? Do you ever seek any feedback from your listeners? If so, do you find such feedback helpful? What could you do to have a more fruitful reflection on your preaching ministry?

SUGGESTED READINGS

Billy, Dennis J. *Plentiful Redemption: An Introduction to Alphonsian Spirituality*. Liguori, Mo.: Liguori Publications, 2001.

________. *With Open Heart: Spiritual Direction in the Alphonsian Tradition*. Liguori, Mo.: Liguori Publications, 2003.

Durwell, Francis X. "To Follow the Example of the Redeemer (Constitution 1): Part I: The Apostolate in Its Deep Dimension." In *Readings in Redemptorist Spirituality*, 4: 94–105. Rome: Redemptorist Spirituality Commission, 1991.

________. "To Follow the Example of the Redeemer (Constitution 1): Part II: By the Missionary Proclamation of the Gospel." In *Readings in Redemptorist Spirituality*, 4:106–17. Rome: Redemptorist Spirituality Commission, 1991.

Gagnon, Jean-Marc, "The Missionary Charism of Saint Alphonsus," *Spiritus Patris* 10 (1984): 87–95.

Hilkert, Mary Catherine. *Naming Grace: Preaching and the Sacramental Imagination*. New York: Continuum, 1997.

I Am Ruined If I Do Not Preach the Gospel (1 Cor 9,16). Communicanda No. 2. Rome: General Curia C.Ss.R., 1999.

Johnstone, Brian. "Saint Alphonsus and the Theology of Conversion." In *Readings in Redemptorist Spirituality*, 2:106–17. Rome: Redemptorist Spirituality Commission, 1988.

Londoño, Noel, ed. *To Be a Redemptorist Today: Reflections on the Redemptorist Charism*. Liguori, Mo.: Liguori Publications, 1996.

Magnier, S.M.. "St. Alphonsus on Preaching," *Search* (1982): 46–51.

Manning, Henry. "The Mission of Saint Alphonsus Liguori." *Spiritus Patris* 16 (1990): 4–22.

Miller, Mark. "The Contribution of Spirituality and Moral Theology in Proclaiming the Word." In *Proceedings of the Fifth International Congress of Redemptorist Moral Theologians, Congress Held in Materdomini, Italy 7–12 July, 2002*, edited by Raymond Douziech, 215–34. Rome: Redemptorist Commission for Moral and Pastoral Theology, 2002.

Miller, Raymond J. "Saint Alphonsus: Extraordinary Missionary Preacher." *Spiritus Patris* 9 (1983): 109–16.

Moran, Terrence James. "Alphonsus Liguori: Preacher of the God of Loveliness." *The Way* 36 (1996): 245–55.

O'Keefe, Mark. "Liturgical Preaching and the Moral Life of Christians." In *Spirituality and Moral Theology: Essays from a Pastoral Perspective*, ed. James Keating, 38–58. New York/Mahwah, N.J.: Paulist Press, 1990.

The Redemptorist Vocation in the Church: The Explicit Proclamation of the Word of God. Communicanda 60, 1981. In *Readings in Redemptorist Spirituality*, 5: 88–105. Rome: Redemptorist Spirituality Commission, 1991.

NOTES

Chapter One

1. Thomas K. Carrol, *Preaching the Word, The Message of the Fathers*, gen. ed. Thomas Halton, vol. 11 (Wilmington, Del., 1984), 21.
2. For more on the history of preaching, see William J. McDonald, gen. ed., *The New Catholic Encyclopedia* (New York: McGraw-Hill, 1967), s.v., "Preaching, I (History of)," by H. Dressler; s.v., "Preaching, II (Homiletic Theory)," by J. M. Connors.
3. For more on Alphonsus's contribution to popular mission preaching, see Louis Châtellier, "La mission populaire: announce prophétique du salut," *Spicilegium historicum CSSR* 45 (1997): 91–111, esp. 100–9.
4. Alphonsus de Liguori, "Prayer, The Great Means of Obtaining Salvation and All the Graces Which We Desire of God" in *The Complete Works of Saint Alphonsus de Liguori,* ed. Eugene Grimm, vol. 3, *The Great Means of Salvation and of Perfection* (Brooklyn/St. Louis/Toronto: Redemptorist Fathers, 1927), 49.

Chapter Two

1. See "Constitution on Simplicity and Manner of Preaching" in *Founding Texts of Redemptorists: Early Rules and Allied Documents,* ed. and trans., Carl Hoegerl (Rome: Collegio Sant' Alfonso, 1986), 341–44.
2. Ibid., 341–42.
3. Ibid., 342.
4. Ibid.
5. Ibid., 342–43.
6. Ibid., 343.
7. Ibid.
8. Ibid., 343–44.

Chapter Three

1. See "Dignity and Duties of the Priest, or Selva" in *The Complete Works of Saint Alphonsus de Liguori,* ed. Eugene Grimm, vol. 12 (Brooklyn/St. Louis/Toronto: Redemptorist Fathers, Centenary edition; reprinted 1927): 19–21, 265–71.
2. Ibid., 19.
3. Ibid., 23–207.
4. Ibid., 208–423.
5. Ibid., 425–71.
6. Ibid., 19–21.
7. Ibid., 265–71.
8. Ibid., 265–88.
9. Ibid., 265.

10. Ibid., 265–66.
11. Ibid., 266–67.
12. Ibid., 268.
13. Ibid., 267–68.
14. Ibid., 269.
15. Ibid.
16. Ibid.
17. Ibid.
18. Ibid., 270.
19. Ibid.
20. Ibid.
21. Ibid.
22. Ibid.
23. Ibid., 265.

Chapter Four

1. See Alphonsus de Liguori, "The Exercises of the Missions" in *The Complete Works of Saint Alphonsus de Liguori,* ed. Eugene Grimm, vol. 15 (New York/Cincinnati/Chicago: Benzinger Brothers, 1890), 91–364.
2. Ibid., 93–94.
3. Ibid., 95–301.
4. Ibid., 302–20.
5. Ibid., 179–253.
6. Ibid., 179–84.
7. Ibid., 184–98.
8. Ibid., 187.
9. Ibid., 188.
10. Ibid., 189–90.
11. Ibid., 198–215.
12. Ibid., 198.
13. Ibid.
14. Ibid., 199.
15. Ibid., 208.
16. Ibid., 215–55.

Chapter Five

1. See "A Letter to a Religious" in *The Complete Works of Saint Alphonsus de Liguori,* ed. Eugene Grimm, vol. 15 (Brooklyn/St. Louis/Toronto: Redemptorist Fathers, Centenary edition; reprinted 1890): 16–62.
2. Ibid., 17.
3. Ibid., 16.
4. Ibid.
5. Ibid., 17–18.
6. Ibid., 19.
7. Ibid., 21.
8. Ibid., 23.
9. Ibid., 23–24.
10. Ibid., 29.
11. Ibid., 52.

12. Ibid., 54.
13. Ibid., 55.
14. Ibid.
15. Ibid., 38.

Chapter Six

1. Alphonsus de Liguori, "Abridged Sermons for All the Sundays of the Year," vol. 16 in *The Complete Works of Saint Alphonsus Liguori,* ed. Eugene Grimm (New York/Cincinnati/Chicago: Benziger Brothers, 1890).
2. Ibid., 53–60.
3. Ibid., 10.
4. Ibid.
5. Ibid., 11–24.
6. Ibid., 53.
7. Ibid.
8. Ibid.
9. Ibid.
10. Ibid.
11. Ibid., 15–16.
12. Ibid., 54.
13. Ibid.
14. Ibid., 55.
15. Ibid., 57
16. Ibid.
17. Ibid., 58.
18. Ibid.
19. Ibid., 59–60.
20. Ibid., 60.
21. Ibid.
22. Ibid., 15.
23. Ibid., 58.

Chapter Seven

1. For the characteristics of Redemptorist preaching, see chapter 2, under the subtitle, "The Characteristics of Redemptorist Preaching" (p. 15).
2. For more on Alphonsus's approach to mental prayer, see Dennis J. Billy, *With Open Heart: Spiritual Direction in the Alphonsian Tradition* (Liguori, MO.: Liguori Publications, 2003), 47–64.
3. See Liguori, "Abridged Sermons," 19.